THE REMINISCENCES OF MARY
Unheard Voices from the Gospels

THE REMINISCENCES OF MARY
Unheard Voices from the Gospels

Peter Corcoran

ATHENA PRESS
LONDON

THE REMINISCENCES OF MARY
Unheard Voices from the Gospels
Copyright © Peter Corcoran 2007

All Rights Reserved

No part of this book may be reproduced in any form
by photocopying or by any electronic or mechanical means,
including information storage or retrieval systems,
without permission in writing from both the copyright
owner and the publisher of this book.

ISBN 10-digit: 1 84401 907 1
ISBN 13-digit: 978 1 84401 907 6

First Published 2007 by
ATHENA PRESS
Queen's House, 2 Holly Road
Twickenham TW1 4EG
United Kingdom

Printed for Athena Press

Contents

Foreword	7
The Happening *Mary's account of her early life and the Annunciation*	8
Mums 'R' Us *Mary's account of her visit to her cousin Elizabeth*	14
The Birthing Shed *Mary's account of the birth of Jesus in Bethlehem*	20
Three Very, Very, Very Wise Men *Mary's account of the Epiphany*	27
Two Excursions *Mary's account of Jesus' presentation in the Temple at forty-days-old and his experience in the Temple aged twelve*	34
The Man Who Went Through the Roof – Literally *The miraculous healing of the man lowered through the roof Told by one of the paralytic's friends*	41
A Blind Man Named Bart *The miracle of the healing of blind Bartimaeus Told by one of Bartimaeus' friends*	47
A Good Year for Chianti *The marriage feast at Cana Told by the Apostle Judas*	53
The Right Place at the Right Time *The feeding of the five thousand Told by the young boy who provided the five loaves and two fish*	59

The Cohens at Number 8   65
The raising of Lazarus
Told by one of the neighbours in the street

First Come, First Served at the Sheep Pool   71
The healing of the man at the sheep pool
Told by a casual observer

Please Call Me Thomas   78
An appreciation of Thomas the Apostle
Told by the various people who knew him throughout his life

A Life Built on Water   93
Incidents from Peter's life
Told by one of his best friends

Foreword

It seems that very shortly after Mary had given birth to her Messiah son in that stable in Bethlehem, the first visitors began to arrive: a group of itinerant shepherds enthusing about a throng of angels singing 'Glory Glory Alleluia'. Possibly all a little too much for Mary to take in at the time. That's why we can see the relevance of those immortal words of Luke: 'she treasured all these things and pondered them in her heart.' Pondered. Stored away for a later time.

Mind you, it is worth pointing out that, as well as being a ponderer, Mary was also a very organised note-taker and diary-keeper. Reminiscences in faintly-lined school exercise books. All neatly written and dated.

It is important we know this. Otherwise we might get the impression that her detailed accounts of the major events of her son's life were the result of a memory that was a little bit more super than natural. Her diligent note-taking was one of her many talents. And how grateful we are for it.

The Happening

Mary's account of her early life and the Annunciation

Extra special

You know, when I think about it, I suppose that over the years one of the most frequent questions I have been asked has been: 'But when did you realise you were extra special?' And it has been a question that has always embarrassed me. I could never really cope with it. I think that is why in the early days I appeared to be a bit flippant, saying things like, 'Well actually from the moment of my birth' or 'After about seven months in the womb'. And, as the Messiah's mother couldn't possibly be flippant, these responses were met with fevered scribbling in spiral-bound notebooks or an adjustment of tape machines so as not to miss any of my pearls of wisdom. Comments like 'Yes, I would imagine so', or, on one occasion, 'How suitably fitting', would be voiced. In my later years, I have tended to be more guarded. And also do fewer interviews.

In the genes

Of course, I did feel special from the word go. Extra special. Anybody with parents like mine would do; they were brilliant. I was their only daughter and they were in their forties when I came along.

You see, Mum had been looking after my grandmother, who was bedridden from quite early on. Dad was, in fact, one of Gran's carers and that is how they met. I often used to think that those genes must have been passed on down the line to Jesus. Because, whatever else he was, our son had real patience and a concern for those who were sick or infirm. But wait a minute, I am jumping a bit. I need to go back to the beginning.

Mary Jay

Like anybody else, I have had to rely on other people's memories for my very early life. Apparently, my first words were 'Abba' and 'Mama', which I am sure doesn't come as a great surprise. The next word was 'Jaja', which was my attempt at 'Marmaduke', our ginger tomcat. Looking back, life seemed just one long holiday of playing with Marmaduke and mothering my favourite doll, Molly. Everything else is rather hazy; but I do remember my first day at Job Street primary school which, despite its name, was really a very happy place. This was in no small part due to Miss Grimston, the head, who had been there for ever. She was great. She knew every child and everything about them and their families. I loved it there. As there were three Marys in our class, she always referred to us using our parent's initials, so I became Mary Jay.

My best friends were Jane, who lived in the next street to us, and her cousin Martha. However, possibly my best friend of all, and I still see him quite a lot, was Matty. He lived next door to us at Number 12 and we really grew up like brother and sister. His mum and dad were a lot younger than mine, so that was nice. Obviously, for a few years at school we cultivated a studied indifference – as you do; but later on we really became close. I still see him from time to time, though he lives in Jericho these days and mends televisions and washing machines.

Bible stories

In the infant school we learned all the basics like reading, writing, adding up and so on, but I don't remember any of it being particularly difficult. Although I was not Mensa standard, I seemed to do all right. It was only in our last few years at school that we did what I would call proper lessons. I always did really well at scripture. Nowadays, reporters always jump on that and say 'Well, of course', but really that is just paper talk. I must admit I got bored with all those lists of rules and laws and also wasn't keen on all the fighting and violence, but I just loved the stories and there were some great ones there. The one about Ruth and that one about Joseph and his psychedelic overcoat I still read over and over again. I also liked the story right at the beginning about God creating the world, Adam and Eve and the serpent and all that; especially that bit about the serpent biting the heel of the man who squashed him to death. I never fully understood it in those days but I found it quite enlightening, really. Hey, listen to me using words like 'enlightening'! Aren't I the clever one?

Chance meeting

Anyway, the top and bottom of it was I left school with everybody else when I was twelve, as you did in those days. I got a part-time job on the checkout at the local supermarket. You see, I don't know whether I mentioned it, but, from the time I was about five, my dad had been more or less housebound. His back had gone with all that lifting and carrying. So once I left school I was able to help out a bit more.

Well, one day I had taken this message from my mum over to Auntie Joanne's and Uncle Ben's. He worked in the Nazareth branch of the Royal Bank of Jerusalem so they had a bit of money. And they were having a new kitchen and dining room suite fitted for them. In cedar. That's when I met Joseph for the first time. Now, although I had never really had all that much to do with mum's side of the family, I suddenly found myself in that part of town more often. And, by chance, I just happened to bump into Joseph on a couple of occasions. He was a nice man, though a bit older than me and fairly quiet; not at all demonstrative. Well, without giving you a blow by blow account of my feminine wiles, he eventually asked me if I would like to go out with him for a coffee. I shyly said, 'Oh, yes please.' So we did, at a nice coffee house that had just opened on Bean Street. I had never thought a cup of coffee could last two hours. Mind you, it was a big cup. And then we arranged to do it again. And again.

Not a good year...

By the time I was approaching my fourteenth birthday, Joseph and I were very much an item and were making grand plans for the future. When would we get married? Where would we live?

How many children would we have? Every day was summer, we were getting on really well, and then things started happening that would change all our lives. Just before my fourteenth birthday in September, my dad took a turn for the worse. He quickly deteriorated and died towards the end of that year. Well, as you can imagine, we were all devastated, I suppose chiefly because we had not realised how poorly he was. We felt horrible. You know, the old Jewish guilt. Mind you, he had a good death and all the people who meant anything to him were present as he quietly slipped away. So that was something. He was buried the very next day, as is our tradition, and we all started to pick up the pieces of our life again as the New Year started.

…Then a better one

And what a year! With winter breathing its last, Joseph asked me to marry him. To be honest, it wasn't completely unexpected but even so it was still such a lovely surprise. I did wonder what Mum would think as she obviously had not really got over Dad's death. But, in the event, she was fine. In fact, her response made me absolutely certain it was the right thing. I found out later that Joseph had mentioned it to her first to see how she felt. That was typical of him; he really was such a lovely man. Also, at this time, Joseph came to live with us. As his home was in Bethsaida, it simply made sense rather than him paying for hotel accommodation. It meant we could prepare for our marriage together and, because we really did love each other, which was obvious to anybody who saw us together, it meant we could be close to each other – without being too close!

Not at all scary

So that was it; until that famous day in spring. Joseph had gone to work. Mum had gone into town. I was chopping up some veg for the chicken casserole I was doing for the evening meal. Suddenly, I got the impression I was not alone. The atmosphere in the kitchen became different. It reminded me of that day some years back when we had an eclipse of the sun. There was a kind of unreal orangey-yellow tinge to the light and there was complete, silent stillness. Even the birds had been gagged. It was eerie but real.

Now, I am a fairly level-headed person, not easily ruffled. Yes, I've got an imagination but it doesn't run away with me. But that day it was like someone was actually talking to me. It wasn't scary or anything; in fact, very much the opposite. There was a kind of massaging voice, putting me at ease, relaxing me. I sat down on the chair that was next to the kitchen table.

Big question, big answer

Such a mishmash of emotions crowded in: curiosity, anxiety, and excitement. Suggestions were in my mind that my God, with whom I had a very down-to-earth conversational relationship, was asking me a very special favour; asking my permission. It didn't quite seem right. Was I prepared to be the mother of the future Messiah, the promised one, the special one, the one our nation had been waiting for? And more: he would actually be the Son of God.

In a funny kind of way, I got the impression that if I had asked 'When will this happen?' I would have got the answer 'Right now'. So I didn't ask. In fact, looking back, I am still surprised how calm I was. I was calm enough to associate my biology lessons from school with my relationship with Joseph and realise that this was a non-starter. Then, as if my thoughts had been noted and accepted, the words, 'He will be the Son of God' were repeated a few times, like a mantra that soothed my mind. And, feeling soothed, I actually said out loud, 'If that's what you want'. Then I had a conversation with myself:

Why?

I don't know.

How?

I don't need to know. But yes.

And then, a bit louder, 'Yes'.

The sun-eclipsed silent stillness slowly disappeared. Things became normal again.

Not me, but us

I remember feeling slightly embarrassed at apparently talking to myself. I made myself a cup of tea and tried to make a bit of sense of what Joseph and I would later call 'the Happening'. And, although even in those early days Joseph and I did not keep secrets from each other, I decided to let things remain as they were for the time being. I felt I had to get my head round this one before I did anything about it. Joseph and I were in a good, honest relationship, with a future marriage very much part of our plans. So, in reality, it was not just me who had been chosen; it was us. I can't tell you how consoling that thought was. Joseph was such a good man. That's why I loved him. That's why it came as no surprise when, a few days later, he came to me and said, 'Darling, I have had an incredible dream about you.'

I was simply able to say, 'No, love. About us.' We hugged each other for some minutes.

Our future together

I suppose it was some days later that we actually sat down and looked at our future together. It was slightly different to our original plans. Also, I had begun to remember other things that the voice had told me. For instance, that Auntie Elizabeth, who was well on in years, was also expecting a baby. I really needed to contact her. But what could I say? 'I have news too. I can more or less tell you what happened. I'm certain it's true. At least, I think so; a kind of definite maybe.'

Does this sound bad? I hope not. It wasn't a question of doubting what had happened; more a question of appreciating what had happened and especially appreciating what had happened to me. To us. I reckoned that would take for ever. But for the moment it meant getting on with our lives. Together. Just us three.

Mums 'R' Us

Mary's account of her visit to her cousin Elizabeth

A new life

It took Mum a few months to get over Dad's death, as you would expect. They had been so happy together. But with me and Joseph she was just brilliant. In the early spring she decided – with no discussion – that we should have two of the rooms in the house as ours. Our own.

'You need your own space,' she said.

And, although it seemed a bit strange at the time, I realised later how wise it was. And that's how we started our life together. We were very happy. We had each other. Though, to be honest, we didn't have a lot else – apart from some very fine handmade furniture; one of the benefits of having a qualified cabinet-maker for a husband. At the time, Joseph was actually working for a local firm that provided flat-pack wardrobes and chairs and things for one of those foreign multi-nationals. But, as he used to say, 'At least it's better than being on the Social.' And, of course, this became even truer with a baby on the way. But it all seemed a little bit unreal.

You know, I don't think I'll ever forget those few weeks as long as I live.

The Happening

First of all, there was what Joseph and I used to refer to as the Happening. Was it real? Was it a dream? And what was 'real'? But that's the trouble with dreams, isn't it? Especially when they deal with things that don't really threaten us. There is always that fine dividing line between where possible reality ends and where real possibility begins. One thing was sure, since the Happening I had

had this definite sense of contentment. We had both slowly come round to accepting the idea of there being an addition to our family.

Mind you, we hadn't told anybody. Apart from Mum. And I definitely wasn't showing. I just kept saying to myself 'I'm going to have a baby and he is to be the Messiah.' I suppose I was mildly hysterical, but at least I wasn't waking Joseph up in the middle of the night with strange food cravings – not as far as I remember, anyway.

The best baby boy

Never having been pregnant before, everything was all so very new. Also, I remember Joseph seemed quieter than usual, more pensive. He said he was happy with the turn of events but I wasn't fully convinced. You know how it is.

One evening, he'd gone out for his usual drink with his friends. He was a real creature of habit, my husband. Every Thursday without fail he met Abe and Josh in The Three Kings. There was nothing worth watching on the TV so I decided to do a bit of tidying up, light stuff like fluffing cushions and making plans. And there, down the side of one of the chairs, I found these drawings. There was a cradle and a nursing chair. Underneath, scribbled in Joseph's scrawly writing was 'For the best baby boy in the whole wide world'. Funny, but I think that's the moment I fully realised we were going to be parents. I never told Joseph I had found the drawings, mind you. I kept it as my secret and his secret. It was a pity, looking back, that we were never able to use the finished items that first year; but we did eventually, and they are still there in the corner of the room as I am writing this.

Your news for my news

But it wasn't just my baby I should have been thinking about. Auntie Elizabeth was supposedly pregnant too. I still feel a little bit ashamed, even after all these years, that we were so taken up with our own news it was some time before I got round to enquiring about her. You see, as you might know, that was part of the angel's message, that she was also expecting. Although, to be fair to myself, that is where the question of whether our Happening was real or a dream got blurred. I mean, pregnant at her age! But anyway, after a few weeks, I eventually did write to her, fairly vaguely, telling her I had some news for her. When I got no answer immediately, I really thought I had put my foot in it. Then, one morning, I remember Joseph calling upstairs: 'Mary! Postcard for you, love.'

There it was; a picture postcard of the Temple at Jerusalem. Not very private, you might think; but, in fact, more than adequate. And such a relief, I can tell you. Next to our address it simply said, 'We all have never been better. Your news for my news. Why not visit?'

Quite a journey

So the following day, after a quick 'Love you, love you, too' farewell (I can't remember actually saying that, but I must have done as that was our usual pet phrase in those days), I set out. It wasn't all that far away but just an awkward place to get to. There used to be a direct train but that had been stopped a few years before. Joseph did offer to drive me there in our newly-acquired Robin Reliant, but I declined, knowing he was keen on getting work done and also unsure as to the wisdom involved in combining three wheels, a bumpy road and my condition. It meant two buses and it was hot and dusty. I actually stood for most of the journey to allow an old man to sit down in a place reserved for 'Elderly passengers and pregnant ladies'. I tell you, I became very tired. The phrase 'I must be pregnant' was buzzing around my mind like a fly in a sweet shop. And, by the time I arrived, I was more than ever convinced it was true. I was shattered, but after a wash and a glass of Pepsi we got down to the serious business of talking.

Quite a first day

I suspect I did most of it; mainly questions. How did she feel? Had she been sick much? What had the neighbours said? How had Uncle Zech taken the news? Had they thought of a name? What about godparents? I was on a roll. Elizabeth answered them all and then went on to tell the story of how Zechariah had been struck dumb and how he still could not speak. The paramedics had transferred him straight away, apparently, to casualty at the Royal Jerusalem Hospital. But, as there was no apparent medical reason for his condition, he had been sent home and told to rest. He was in the bedroom as we were talking.

You know, that first day we must have drunk gallons of tea all served, as I remember, out of delicate china mugs. And the teapot! I can still see it. It was in the shape of the High Priest's Palace. Apparently, it was part of a set produced for some jubilee or other. I also remember Elizabeth making some comment like: 'I suppose tea will have to do, though to be honest, love, I could murder a gin and tonic!'

Actually, I was quite happy with tea, myself. I've never been a great drinker. I liked a small glass of sherry on my birthday, but that was all.

Messiah fever

Elizabeth explained that communication with Uncle Zech was pretty difficult but they were getting by with him using some kind of magic board that he wrote on with a special pen and then rubbed clean. One of the younger priests had apparently got it from the market. And then, somehow, we got round to the fact that the two of them believed that, because of everything that had gone on, they thought perhaps their baby might be special; although not a priest or anything like his father, because that was more of a family or tribal thing. Recently, there had been an upsurge in Jerusalem of what could only be called 'Messiah fever' and they had wondered whether their baby might have something to do with that: a helper, or maybe even the Messiah himself. Elizabeth said she knew that sounded ridiculous but presumably he had to be born to someone, so why not them? They had a good religious pedigree.

The right time?

I can still remember, no 'remember' is too little a word, I was overcome by... I was avalanched by what we were talking about.

It was crazy, the way the conversation had gone. I mean, I know I wasn't sworn to secrecy or anything, and I had been wondering when would be the best time to break my news, but now it seemed the decision had been taken for me. I was a little bit hesitant; but in the end I decided just to go for it, and it all bubbled out about the Happening and how I had explained to the voice immediately that being a mother was not really an option for me if what I had learned in biology at school was true. I had actually got a B in my GCSE. And then I went on about what I had been told about my son – that he was to be a special one; in fact, he was to be the Messiah.

Suddenly very young

I wonder if you can possibly imagine how I felt? Here we were, two mothers-to-be; one pretty old and one pretty young; one by all normal circumstances beyond the age of child-bearing and me at the beginning of my child-bearing career; one special, one everyday ordinary; one living in a grace-and-favour home with her elderly Temple priest husband, one still at her mother's with a redundant cabinet-maker husband. After I finished my story, the silence was deafening. The clock ticked on maximum. I didn't know what to expect. I was kind of frightened, kind of nervous, and feeling very young. Then Elizabeth looked at me and spoke, very quietly. I can remember the words as if she were saying them here now: 'Perhaps gin and tonic is not a good idea but I have some lemonade in the fridge.' And then we started laughing and crying all over each other.

After this, on top of the journey and the excitement, I was ready for bed. We both were. After all, as Elizabeth said, we were now sleeping for four.

Two special babies...

Over the next few weeks we had some terrific, fantastic, unreal conversations. We made ridiculous plans, some of which came true. We talked about whether Joseph and I would have to move, when we would tell people, what the neighbours would think. And then we broadened the net to lateral thinking and horizontal thinking and all compass points in between. And not just about my Messiah; we both decided that pretty early on. No, this was not just about me. We shouldn't cloud the fact that Elizabeth's baby was obviously going to be somebody very special as well. Everything about the circumstances suggested that. But what? Well, as we both agreed, our God did not do coincidences or chance. So, possibly, as we were tied by blood maybe our children would be tied by vocation or work or something. We had some great times working out various scenarios and also some wonderfully silly times. According to some of the prophets, the Messiah was going to be a warrior king, so perhaps Elizabeth's son could look after my son's horse. Or in a time of milk and honey someone would have to be marketing manager.

…Two special grown-ups

Then we got more sensible and down to earth and ordinary and more like ourselves. I remember Elizabeth saying it would be great if her son – they hadn't thought of a name yet – could help his cousin. That way, at least, they would be able to start from a point of trust and not have to earn it like when you are working with strangers. And that's how it was for the next few weeks. We discussed the future. We conceived grand ideas for our two children, separated in age by a few months. They would change the world, working together. The possibilities were unlimited.

A special winter

The time flew by and, as Elizabeth became more blooming, I started to show the early stages of a bump. I was proud, I was happy, I was tired, and a little bit lonely. In fact, to be fair, I was really looking forward to getting back home. I was missing Joseph. True, we had been in touch by phone or text most days, but it was not the same; and I knew he was missing me. And also we had some preparing to do. This was going to be a very special winter for us.

The Birthing Shed

Mary's account of the birth of Jesus in Bethlehem

Home to Joseph

My stay at Elizabeth's was just perfect. We had a great time together and between us managed to sort our heads out, but I was glad to get home. The bus got into Nazareth about half past four. Well, if you'd seen Joseph sprint across that tarmac! His bear hug put back in place any joints or bones displaced by the bumpy journey, and then he stood back and looked me up and down and said: 'You look great, love.'

Now, unless you knew Joseph, that might seem quite low key. But for him it was a lot. It was at least equivalent to a couple of love sonnets dripping from the lips of that English playwright Shakespeare. That night we simply wrapped ourselves round each other and a Chinese take-away and talked and listened and enjoyed being together again. I realised, not for the first time, how lucky I was having Joseph. And in the coming months this feeling was really going to be reinforced.

On the move

It was still early in the summer and the baby wasn't due until the winter but there was a definite air of expectancy in our house. I was growing larger by the day (or, at least, felt I was), and Joseph was growing greyer. But, since the Happening, nothing really out of the ordinary had occurred; unless you count the fairly vivid dream Joseph had had assuring him things would be all right. So we decided it was up to us to get our act together regarding any preparations. Top of the list: somewhere else to live. Even if we only had this one special child, we really did need a place of our own. So during the autumn we moved into this lovely little three bedroom terraced house in Fisher Street.

On the move again

Before we had time to settle in, this very official-looking letter arrived, redirected from Mum's house in Bethany Close. The first half was information. The powers that be in Rome had decided that they would like to have a census of all the people who were living in their 'accommodation areas'. Joseph suggested that it should really have read 'occupied zones', but anyway.

It would be different for each country. For some it would be a postal census. Others would report to their nearest major city. But the Jews, 'because of your thoroughly commendable respect for your religious ethnic history', would have to go to 'the family town of your patriarch'. The date for the census was the last two weeks of the year. A list was given and we were to report to the town allotted to those of the House of David – Bethlehem.

Early nomadic training

We looked down the sheet for any possible exceptions. Children under two years of age did not have to register. Elderly people over ninety were excused the journey, as were pregnant women beyond six months – but not their partners. It would mean a long journey but I was not keen on being separated from Joseph again, so we decided we would both go. As there was a brand-new NHS Trust hospital just outside Bethlehem, if there were any complications with the birth I could always go there. And, as we had not really settled into our new home, we could make a whole new start when we returned. We also decided we would set off in good time and make it a bit of a holiday. As you know, we Jews had always been a bit of a nomadic people so we felt it would be good for the future Messiah to get a taste of travelling about.

Ned

And of course there was Ned. Now, though some neighbours – even new ones – might not mind looking after a cat or even feeding a budgie or a goldfish, some draw the line at a donkey. I won't go into details but just let it be said we had acquired Ned in lieu of payment for a fitted kitchen Joseph had put in. Strange?

Don't ask. But we were very positive and decided a trip by donkey would be very romantic and give us quality time together.

'Just you see what Ned looks like when I have finished with him,' Joseph said.

Well, I'm not kidding you. Have you have ever seen those pictures of the raja in India perched on what looked like an upholstered elephant? Well, that was me, just a bit closer to the ground. Have small house, will travel. So we did. Though, because of the traditional hospitality of the country people, it did take longer than we bargained for, especially once people realised I was pregnant. We eventually trundled into Bethlehem just as winter was starting to bite hard.

Simply no room

Well, as you can imagine, the place was heaving. Joseph traipsed from house to house and hotel to hotel and even bungalow to bungalow, but there was simply no room. I really felt so sorry for him. What a love. He had been brilliant all along. He was so supportive, he never grumbled and never asked why; and now this. I could see he was becoming a little downcast; and, to be honest, I was beginning to wonder a bit myself. Why was there no room? This was the Messiah, after all. Their Messiah. These were his people. Possibly it was me, because I was so blatantly pregnant by this time. Or was it Ned? Some people are funny with animals. I decided that God must have some good reason for the situation. I only wish I could have seen it.

Then our luck changed. I can still see that look in my husband's eye: a kind of guarded optimism, qualified success. It turned out that the chap who owned the Bethlehem Station Hotel had some stables. They'd not been used for some time but they were clean and dry and there was running water. Plus we could use the toilet facilities of the hotel. And it was free. The only possible drawback was an old ox in the next stable. So that was it, just as described in the brochure: clean en suite stable. The ox was actually more in our place than his own, as the wall was non-existent, but we could live with that.

Friends in need

There were actually five stables in all and the others soon became occupied, which was good, really, because we made friends. It became quite a little commune with people plucked from all over the place. Martha, a nurse, and Pete, her husband, an electrician, became our really good friends. We still see them. So we all settled in quite comfortably. I was amazed what Joseph had managed to fit onto our travelling donkey, who, incidentally, seemed to have struck up quite a friendship with the ox. As the days rolled by, nothing was said about when and where to register. So we just sat tight, waiting for information. Mind you, as you can imagine, I had other things on my mind besides the census.

Late night, early morning

It was in the middle of a freezing winter's night that I had a feeling something was happening that was different from my earlier bouts of sickness. I called Martha across from her stable and she said that, as far as she could see, I was 'well on'. She immediately began to organise people. Joseph and Pete were dispatched to get some hot water. I was made comfortable on my bed, lying back like one of those nomadic desert chiefs beloved of old Hollywood movies. Maria – another of our neighbours – suddenly turned up with some white baby sheets and, with an artistic flourish, changed what had been a redundant old feeding trough with wobbly legs into a very fine ethnic cradle. Somebody produced a CD player and some mood music. Then, at more or less quarter past two the next morning, after an experience impossible to explain, Martha's exclamation 'It's a boy' echoed round the stable. I was a mixture of relief and enjoyment and tiredness and everything else positive. It was only later that I got a little bit apprehensive, but at that moment the world was a great place.

Our baby – and us

After a couple of hours, the others went back to their own stables and we were left alone. We were a happy, contented, nervous threesome: one exhausted woman, one relieved man, and one very hungry baby; ours. As I lay back with the two most important people in my life near me, the whole nine months came flooding back. It was a real mixture of emotions and feelings: the strange other-worldliness of the famous Happening, with my faith-driven freedom to believe it would all come true if I said yes; the growing appreciation of my husband's trust in me and in God and in our new-born responsibility; the bubbling warmth of Elizabeth and our manic hilarity as we tried to second-guess our God in his plans for our sons; and then the journey and the birth. It was all a little too much. So I cried. Not the salty, sad tears of a questioning 'why me?' No. They were the baby-soft tears of an accepting 'yes, me'.

First visitors

However, this snug, cuddly, wrapped-round peace did not last too long. I suddenly got the impression we were not alone. I nudged Joseph, who woke up with a start. There, looking round the door of the stable, was a dusky, cold face with straggly, uncombed hair; a boy of maybe eight. He spoke. 'Are you the one with the special baby, missus?' he said.

Well, what do you say? Suddenly, he was joined by three others, all a bit older than him, with similar complexions and similar haircuts. The leader, I suppose a young lad of about sixteen or so, came shyly forward and placed a new-born lamb at my feet. 'That's for the special baby, missus. From us.' Now my experience of new-born lambs was on a par with my experience of new-born babies but the two new-borns looked just right together: the shepherds' offering next to my own little lamb. Joseph thanked them for their kind expensive gift.

Hilltop message

The shepherds went on to explain how they had been sitting round their fire on the hills overlooking Bethlehem when a clock chimed and suddenly above them appeared a kind of bright light with strange music and a voice telling them about a baby in a stable; but not just any baby, a special one. And, although none of them had ever seen a ghost, they knew this was not one because they felt so calm and happy.

We offered them a cup of tea and we chatted. They seemed a little bit disappointed there was not a lot we could tell them about our special baby. Then they left and wished us well and thanked us for the tea. They were nice young people, really genuine.

Time to go

And that was about it. We eventually got round to filling in the forms for the census and decided to make our way home. We were obviously very conscious of our new responsibility but, as we weren't getting any heavenly instructions, we still presumed we must be doing the right thing. As we said at the time, our new baby Messiah had two good parents who loved each other and loved him. We weren't particularly rich but Joseph now had a good job and I hoped to go back to college after our baby got a bit older. We couldn't do any more.

We stayed on in Bethlehem for a few more weeks, mainly to find out as much as we could first-hand about our baby's ancestors and things like that. It seemed a shame to miss the opportunity.

Back home

We gave Ned and the lamb away to a local orphanage in Bethlehem, which was mainly for children whose parents had been killed in the various wars that always seemed to be going on in that part of the world. As you can imagine, they were thrilled.

We got the bus back home to start again our new life together in our new house. Everything seemed so normal. To the people in Fisher Street we were just another young couple starting the next stage of their life together bringing up their new-born baby boy. To us, I suppose, looking back, that is also just how we saw ourselves.

Three Very, Very, Very Wise Men

Mary's account of the Epiphany

Surprise visitors

This is the story of when three wise men stayed with us overnight in our three bedroom house in Fisher Street, East Nazareth. I suppose Jesus must have been about eighteen months old at the time. He'd had all the various tests and, as far as anyone could tell, he was a normal healthy baby. He was the right size for his weight and, if he'd had a passport, we would have ticked the box which said 'no distinguishing features'.

Suddenly, out of the blue one morning, our doorbell rang. Joseph answered it, came back into the house and, in a low conspiratorial voice, said: 'Darling, have you ordered three camels with a wise man sitting on each?'

I remember saying something like 'Not three'. Then I realised he was serious. They didn't immediately introduce themselves as 'wise men'. Mind you, that was possibly a good thing because it would have made us a little bit suspicious. Wise men would not normally be out travelling at midday in our part of the world. However, our traditions required we offer them hospitality, so we did. One of them introduced himself as Melchior ('But you can call me Mel!') and went on to explain that they were from further out east and had been travelling for some months, following a star that they had picked up not far from Babylon. It had apparently wavered a bit over Bethlehem, but then moved on. They had completely lost sight of it on the outskirts of Jerusalem due to fumes from a big chemical fire. It was then that they had decided to ask for directions.

Dubious interest

They'd gone to the Temple to ask if anybody knew where the Messiah was to be found. I remember this mention of 'Messiah' caused Joseph and I to sneak a glance at each other, but we let Mel continue. Apparently, the duty priest had told them that it was really a question for the High Priest, who was unfortunately away for a fortnight, at his holiday home near the Sea of Galilee. As no suitable religious voice could be found, they eventually found themselves in front of Herod who didn't seem to know what they were talking about, but suggested that if they did have any luck they should return to inform him where the Messiah was so he could pay his respects in an appropriate way. It all sounded a bit shady to them, so they were quite relieved to see the star again that night, which eventually stopped over our house. And that was it.

House guests

Well, we didn't quite know what response to make. Their story seemed plausible but it took us a bit by surprise. So we played for time and showed them where the bathroom was and Joseph explained that, as long as they were in Nazareth, they were more than welcome to stay with us. We had a couple of spare bedrooms if they didn't mind sharing. They said this would be fine; they had brought sleeping bags and were quite used to roughing it. I was going to point out that the rooms were just decorated so it wouldn't be a question of 'roughing it' but decided not to diffuse the generous atmosphere created by my husband.

Then Melchior spoke up again. He suggested that before they got down to the real reason for their visit there was one thing they would like to clear up. He wanted to know what kind of area this was, as he wondered if their camels would be safe. My reply that camel rustling had more or less died out with the advent of the supermarket met with a blank response. I remember wondering whether this was an example of humour not travelling. It was agreed they could use our backyard as a stable.

Whose Messiah?

Having cleared up that point, Melchior, who seemed to be the leader, suddenly said: 'And now we come to the chief point of our being here: to worship the Messiah'. And then, like one of those television magicians, he produced three small, highly decorated boxes from somewhere. They were each a different colour and contained gold, frankincense and myrrh. I felt a speech coming on and was not disappointed.

'We would like to present these souvenirs from our three countries. Meaningful souvenirs. Universal gifts for a universal Messiah.'

You know, even after all these years, those words still send a cold tingling down my spine. Here were these three foreigners making a public proclamation of something Joseph and I were stumblingly trying to get our heads round: the vocation of our special child.

Our Messiah

There was another problem: the Jewish dimension. Joseph and I were Jews. Jesus was a Jew. He had already taken part in the Jewish ceremonies of Circumcision and Presentation. Our understanding, sketchy though it was, was that he was the Jewish Messiah. So this pretty blunt statement from this visiting wise Oriental did take us a little bit off-guard. I remember saying, in a fairly light-hearted way, 'Well, actually, he is our Messiah so possibly you might have to get your own. But you can leave the gifts if you wish.' There was a stunned, lead balloon silence, which maybe again hinted at humour not having a passport. Then Joseph, bless him, suggested we should discuss this misunderstanding over a nice cup of tea. I presume it was him who suggested it because that is what he was like and I was probably too uptight anyway.

Jacob's Creek and red socks

Actually, we did more than patch things up. It was time for Jesus' feed, after which I would put him down for the night. We suggested that our three visitors should go for a bit of a walk to stretch their legs and take in the sights of East Nazareth and we would have a meal prepared for about 7 o'clock, if that was all right. This met with their approval and gave us a bit of time together, just to chew over where we were in our Messiah-rearing programme. I remember asking Joseph how he felt and he said that it was a little bit like being a bright red sock in a washing machine full of whites. Always there, but only every now and again thrust into view. To this day I am not sure what he meant but it sounded good and it did express in a funny kind of way how we did seem to be coming to the notice of unexpected people at unexpected times: shepherds in Bethlehem, Simeon and Anna in Jerusalem, and now three camel-riding wise men from the Orient. And our baby was still only eighteen months old.

Jesus was safely in bed by the time the lasagne was cooked and our guests returned with a couple of bottles of Jacob's Creek, which was very good of them. We sat down to eat and talk and enjoyed a very pleasant evening together.

Cryptic web-message

I tried to apologise a bit for my earlier attempts at humour but they brushed them away in a very kind sort of way. They went on to explain that really they were the ones who should feel guilty. They explained to us just how they came to be sitting there in our living room. Apparently, each had been studying their sacred books and, independently, at more or less the same time had discovered a reference to a different kind of star. It was Melchior who first posted it on his website with a simple message: 'Special star follower? Babylon. Spring bank holiday. Be there.'

Balthazar and Caspar had picked up on it. The rest is history.

Good honest discussion

I remember we talked long into the night. The food and drink helped to thaw any of the initial suspicions we had had. It was interesting, really: Jesus was upstairs asleep in his bedroom while we, downstairs, talked in general terms about our ideas of a Messiah – what he would bring to the world and what we needed saving from, things like that. To be honest, we skirted round the actual status of the Messiah regarding the Jewish nation and other nations. Joseph and I had decided, while our guests were out for their walk, that we really were out of our depth on that one. Sure, we'd both studied scripture at school – in fact, Joseph had done it at college – but this was different. On this topic, we needed advice.

Our guests went to bed about midnight and we didn't stay up long after that, just cleared up the plates and glasses. It really had been a very pleasant evening, though we knew we were on the verge of something important in the life of our baby Messiah. No doubt later in his life he would have to be a man of choice, but at this stage it was up to us.

Good honest people

Our three guests wisely slept late and leisurely ate a full Jewish breakfast at round about 11 o'clock. They apologised for leaving so soon, but they all had to be back for the beginning of the university term. Their decision not to pay Herod a return visit meant quite a long detour. They thanked us for our hospitality and went on their way, promising to keep in touch.

And, to be fair, they have done. In fact I got an e-mail only the other day from Caspar, just bringing me up to date with his news. They're such nice people. It's funny isn't it, when you think? We were brought up as children with terms like 'gentile' and even 'heathen' but when you actually meet and talk with these people those words seem really out of place.

Informed information

The next afternoon at half past three saw us all in the Chief Rabbi's office. Our baby was fast asleep in his new papoose, a present from his paternal grandmother. You know, even at this distance, it is strange looking back at that meeting. We briefly explained about our three visitors and our conversation late into the night – we didn't mention the Jacob's Creek or that the topic of conversation had been the promised Messiah. We steered a pretty wide berth around ourselves and our baby but rather took on the mantle of concerned parents, especially in the light of the multi-cultural world we felt our child would be growing up in. Joseph did most of the talking and I remember him asking whether or not there was anything written that each nation had to have its own Messiah or if there was a shared one for everybody.

Well, at this there was a bit of beard scratching before the Chief Rabbi spoke up. He explained that his understanding was that the Messiah would come to one particular race. 'And our belief, as children of Abraham, is that he will come to us.'

He explained that, as far as he knew, reference to a Messiah could be found in the sacred writings of other religions but the evidence was not as strong as ours. Then he stopped, as if that was it.

But what if?

I think he was a bit surprised when Joseph continued and asked if there was any evidence in history of a nation refusing to accept its Messiah. The rabbi said there was nothing according to his knowledge. Joseph persevered and asked what would happen if did happen. Eventually, having consulted a couple of the others, he said that he presumed, in theory, it was possible but really it would be very silly. I remember him saying something like: 'Take our case, for example. Show me any good Jew who would not wish to be rid of the Romans?' This was generally agreed upon and, with smiles all round, we were ushered out, but not before one quite elderly rabbi spoke up. 'But don't forget, my children, you never know what human beings will do. We are a funny lot.'

'Yes' of faith and 'Yes' of trust

That evening, as we sat in our visitor-free front room with Jesus fast asleep upstairs, we really felt very tired. It had been such a hectic couple of days, giving us some real food for thought. We had often wondered whether we were doing the right thing by our son. Yet though we were not receiving divine messages on the mobile or envelopes postmarked 'Heaven' through the letterbox, we were becoming increasingly aware of the constant tips and nudges we were being given. These three camel-riding wise men from the Orient were just the latest. It was slowly dawning on us that the 'Yes' of faith I had given at the Happening was nothing to compare with the 'Yes' of trust that God was placing in us to read the signs and to recognise the hints as we educated our son to be the Messiah the world was waiting for.

Two Excursions

Mary's account of Jesus' presentation in the temple at forty-days-old and his experience in the temple aged twelve

Growing fast

As Jesus graduated from Pampers to Baby-Gro to Mothercare denim outfits, there was nothing really to set him apart. By and large, nobody guessed he was anyone special because, by and large, there was nothing he did that was special.

In fact, there were only a couple of occasions when anybody, even with a perceptive mind, might suspect anything was different. I admit that visit by those three wise men from the Orient was a bit out of the ordinary, but most people in our town just seemed to regard them as exotic visitors who had lost their way and just happened on us and enjoyed our hospitality for a time.

Forward planning

Having returned from Bethlehem, we were soon back on our travels again. This time we went to Jerusalem, to present our son. If our stable experience had taught us anything, it was the value of forward planning, especially as we now had a young baby to care for, one who needed feeding and changing and space to cry and whinge and be an ordinary baby. So we booked in advance to stay a couple of nights at this nice little bed and breakfast run by Mrs Gold. We arrived late on Wednesday evening and went straight to bed.

A special garden

On the Thursday we went to the Temple to find out the details for the following day. We really had no clue what to expect. One of our neighbours had said: 'The chief thing is to make sure you have a couple of pigeons. And you get them cheaper at the market than in the Temple forecourt.' That was all we knew.

So we went to the Temple, where we were given a pamphlet and told to attend at door B14 with our pigeons and our baby at 3 o'clock the following afternoon. Fortunately, Jesus was pretty regular with his feeds so this time suited us. That afternoon we did a little bit of sight-seeing and then, early that evening, had a pleasant walk round the Garden of Gethsemane, which was quite close to Mrs Gold's. It really was a beautiful place, with the olive trees and palms and things. It was all very peaceful and relaxing, quite prayerful, really. But as I was still a little bit tired with the events of the last month or so, we didn't stay out too long.

The words of another of our neighbours came to mind: 'Now don't you rush things, Mary. Having a baby is not like having a tooth out, you know. Your body takes time to readjust.' Like most old wives, she was so right.

Presentation

On the Friday, we arrived at room B14 in plenty of time. And, exactly at 3 o'clock, a priest came out and introduced himself as Rabbi Abimelech. He asked us to follow him as he led the way to an altar of sacrifice. Here he explained that the first ceremony would be one of purification for me, in keeping with the traditional Jewish teaching that any loss of blood made a woman unclean. He prayed over me and then anointed my head. My response of 'Amen, Alleluia' was greeted with a simple nod. Then he held Jesus as we both read from a card: 'We consecrate to God our baby, Jesus, forty days old, as a sign of thanksgiving for his birth and also of our people's deliverance from the Pharaoh. We promise to bring up our son to keep God's law and, as a further sign of gratitude, we present these two pigeons to God.'

Rabbi Abimelech gave Jesus back to us, accepted our gift and thanked us and blessed us and wished us a safe journey back to our home. And that was it. We went outside and found a bench in the corner of a little walled garden and sat down to recover, to relax, and to privately, as a family, give thanks to God for this significant moment in our child's life. We reflected on the irony: and privilege of offering to God the baby whom God had offered to us. The sheer mystery contained in the ordinariness of the baby in the white bundle was more powerful than any artist could paint or any writer could describe. We just felt incredibly lucky and thankful for our God, our child, our family.

A special old man

Just as we were making our way out to get back to Mrs Gold's, this elderly man – and I mean really old – shuffled towards us. He looked first at Joseph, then at me, and then at Jesus snuggled tightly in his fluffy white shawl. 'It is, isn't it?' he said.

Joseph looked at me and I looked at Joseph and we both muttered 'Probably'.

Then he suddenly said: 'If you only knew how long I have been waiting for this moment! I feel I can die in peace now. Do you mind if I hold him?'

Well, to be honest, I wasn't all that keen because, even though Jesus was so small, he was still a bit of a handful when he wriggled about. Proper little eel he was. But we thought: *Well, why not?* So I sat on one side of him and Joseph sat on the other, both poised like slip fielders at a Test match. The old man just looked into Jesus' eyes and then at us and repeated what he had said earlier about being ready to die. We both thought he was just a bit old and was forgetting what he had said earlier, but no way; this was no rambling old man...

A special message

He went on to explain to us that, as far as he was concerned, he was holding the very promise that God had made and kept with the whole world. 'This baby, your baby,' he said, 'proves that God has kept his promise that he would save everybody, Jews and non-Jews alike.' Then he turned to us and asked us if we knew what a special baby we had.

Well, we didn't want to give too much away so we just agreed how special he was to us. He picked up on this and explained that indeed this was a special baby, but it wouldn't all be plain sailing. To be honest, I can't remember his exact words, but he did talk about Jesus being someone who would make friends but also a lot of enemies.

'Some people can't cope with the truth, you know,' he said. And then he turned to me and used a phrase that still sticks with me: 'And a sword will pierce your own heart, too, my dear.'

A special old lady

Then he gave Jesus back to us. But, as we made to go, we found our path blocked by a little wizened eighty-four-year-old lady – it turned out it was her birthday that day. She said first of all that what Simeon, because that was the old man's name, had said was true. But she also told us not to be worried because the good we would experience in our lives would far outweigh the bad. She then walked away, at a remarkable speed for her age, down this kind of cloister and was shouting that the wait was over and the Messiah was born. As it happened, not a lot of people listened to her and we were able to make our way out after a very exhausting couple of days. We were physically and mentally shattered, and really looking forward to getting back home.

Painful reminder

Now I just want to digress a bit. As you know, the title of this story is 'Two Excursions'. And I had the notes just to continue with number two: the time we travelled up to Jerusalem for the first time with Jesus as a young adult and we lost him. But something quite significant happened only yesterday. I was in the local supermarket and suddenly over the tannoy came: 'Would Mrs Lipman please go to the information desk to collect her daughter Martha.' Well, I tell you, it suddenly all came back. My notes reminded me that we lost Jesus but that tinny voice reminded me how horrific it was. It really helped me to descale my memory of the day we mislaid the young Messiah.

Part boy, part man

You probably know the situation. How each year Joseph and I used to go up to Jerusalem for a couple of days for special prayers, a short pilgrimage round ancient shrines and things like that. We found it did us good; a real spiritual pick-me-up. Previously we had left Jesus with Joseph's mother, but this year we took him with us. He was twelve years old, so kind of officially an adult. Not that he acted like one. But anyway, after a couple of days we made our way back home. The tradition was that the women and children travelled in one group, the men in the other. It was only when we got to the bus station at Sychar, in Samaria, that we realised Jesus was not with us. It was a total mix-up. I presumed he was with the men because he almost was one. Joseph presumed he was with us and the children because he was, likewise, still a child. Anyway, the top and bottom of it was we had to return. The last bus had gone to Jerusalem and there seemed to be a total absence of taxis. And, as we wanted to make sure we got away as soon as possible the next morning, we decided to stay in the waiting room. Well you can imagine what a night that was. That's why that supermarket announcement brought me out in such a cold sweat.

An unconditional yes

As I mentioned before, I had always felt slightly apprehensive whether we were bringing Jesus up the right way for the future Messiah. Now don't get me wrong, I never really had any doubts about my original 'Yes', but when I said 'Yes' to God I didn't say 'No' to me. I still remained the same person, warts and all. And although in my saner, non-emotional moments I realised that my faith had in fact got stronger over the years, nonetheless, when things appeared not to be quite going according to plan, it was then that darker feelings seemed to worm their way in. It was then I would have appreciated the odd heavenly direction or divine e-mail. And, of course, this was never more so than when we quite simply realised we had lost our son. Rock bottom and snake's insteps possibly summed up how low we felt during that night in the bus station at Sychar.

Grown-up child

We arrived back in Jerusalem just before midday and started to retrace our steps, eventually finishing up in the area around the Temple where teachers and scholars gave talks and courses on various aspects of scripture. And there, large as life, was our son, sitting with a group of other young adults. He was totally focused. We resisted the temptation to rush across to him and ask him what he was doing. We didn't want to be overbearing parents with a cool adolescent. So we held back and just listened. To be honest we both felt quite proud as we noticed the intelligent and polite way he was joining in the sessions. It also suddenly dawned on us how grown-up he had become. I suppose constantly being with each other in everyday, familiar circumstances you tend not to notice change too much.

Two points of view

Eventually, they stopped for a break. We took Jesus to one side and explained how worried we had been and questioned him as to why he hadn't told us that he was staying behind. He apologised for any upset he had caused but he also said that we had to see his point of view. We all knew that God had something special in mind for him and therefore he felt that this was too good an opportunity to miss, with these special teachers and lecturers in town for the festival. As we were talking, a couple of these same teachers came past and one of them said to us: 'You've got a bright lad there, you know.' And then to Jesus: 'Well done, son. Keep up the study because I think you have the makings of someone special.' Both Joseph and I thanked the man and were pleased that Jesus accepted the compliment gracefully, in quite a mature way. We then made our way back home.

Birth of a young man

It was funny, really, because this was a real growth point in all our lives. What could have been a real negative event, with loss and disagreement, was actually a blossoming. We came to appreciate our importance to each other, especially relevant in so far as, within nine months, Joseph was dead. He caught a virus; such a small word for such an enormous effect, such a loss. He was such a man, with so much wisdom and so much insight. I can still remember our last conversation just before he died. We'd been discussing losing Jesus those few months earlier and he simply looked at me and said: 'You don't need to worry you know, love. This old man might be dying, but another younger one is being born.'

He was a good man, my Joseph; so wise. I still miss him.

The Man Who Went Through the Roof – Literally

The miraculous healing of the man lowered through the roof
Told by one of the paralytic's friends*

An easy job?

I suppose really we should never have taken the job on, but you know what it's like when there's no work and you're hungry. Mind you, if we had refused it, I suppose things would have been a bit different. Well, I wouldn't be telling you this story for a start. I suppose, to be fair, more good than bad did come out of it. Did I say 'I suppose'?

All in a day's work

You see, there were five of us. We were a team. And these two Pharisees had asked us to paint this sepulchre. White. I preferred green myself, but a job's a job. It was on a contract basis, four days, no overtime. So we had to get a move on. But mix high walls and short ladders and you have a recipe for disaster. Simon fell and never walked again. Not to this day. No, I tell a lie, not until yesterday. You see it still hasn't really sunk in yet. But anyway, to get back to the story, there was this terrific crack. Well, I knew the ladder was finished. But worse, Simon just lay there. He was dead still, but fortunately still alive. We could hear him groaning in real pain, but we still just waited for him to get up. Well, you do, don't you? We expected him to dust himself down and apologise for breaking Paul's ladder; but no. This was for real.

---

* This story can be found in Luke, chapter five.

Teamwork

So, anyway, we used the smaller bit of the ladder as a kind of stretcher and rushed him to a physician, who gave him some drug or other which put him to sleep. He then told us that things did not look good. Well, we knew that, but it is sometimes easier to hear bad news from someone with authority, isn't it? He gave us some other things to help Simon when he came round. When I say 'give', I mean we did a deal. He gave us medicine, we gave him money. Not that we begrudged any of it. And that is honest. I mean, we were a team.

Trying everything

You see, every time we looked at Simon we realised it could quite easily have been Josh or Luke or any of us. I mean nothing was broken or anything – like arms or legs or things – it was just something had gone in his back.

'Spinal cord,' said that first physician. 'Keep him lying down.' And, to be fair, Jude really made that ladder into quite a neat and comfortable stretcher. I mean, it was obvious it had once been a ladder but, with a bit of padding and rubber on the ends, it was perfect. Well, nearly. Luke also said it was a good job there were five in our team or else we would have had to co-opt someone as a stretcher bearer. He's always been one for dry humour has Luke. Well, we took Simon all over on that stretcher, to different doctors and physicians and the like. We even tried a witch on one occasion, but that is just between us and I'd prefer you didn't mention it to anybody else. But we had no luck. And poor old Simon was losing heart himself.

When all else fails

Then, the day before yesterday, we heard that this man, Jesus, was going to be in Capernaum the following day. Well, none of us is particularly religious but we had all heard of Jesus. Who hadn't? Also, as he himself was not regarded as particularly religious by the authorities, we felt we had something in common. Anyway, the long and short of it was that we decided to give it a try. As

Luke said, we had been to the official medical people and this was like trying alternative medicine. Nobody really understood that, sometimes Luke can be too dry. Well, we mentioned it to Simon. You know, I can still see him looking up at me and saying: 'Laz, must I?'

I just said, 'Yes, Simon. I think that we should give it one more go.' And I explained that Jesus had a good success rate on healing. It was difficult because we were never sure whether we were doing all this running about for Simon's good or because we ourselves felt a bit guilty. It wasn't easy, if you know what I mean?

Time for action

Anyway, early yesterday, with our stretcher charged up and with Simon on board, we set off for Capernaum. We made good time and soon we were at the house where Jesus was visiting. Well, I say 'at the house' but I mean outside. There was no chance that we would get in. The place was heaving. The queues were coming out of the house like toothpaste coming out of a tube.

Luke suggested we try the 'Excuse me, stretcher' technique but we could see we weren't the only ones in that situation. Well, I must admit, at this point I was all for coming home. We had done our best. Nobody could have done more. And, to be fair, Simon looked all in. It was then that the thought flashed through my mind. Perhaps he was not just having a bad day. Perhaps things had got too much for him. Perhaps he was very seriously ill. Part of me felt bad for persuading him to come. The other part was more determined than ever to put our whole hope in this Jesus.

Bright idea

Luke, I noticed, was looking blank. This is usually a sign of deep thought with him. As well as his dry humour, he is also the philosopher in the group. They're not always practical but he's brimful of ideas. Actually, it was him who had got the sepulchre contract. Now, he was looking at the roof and stroking an imaginary beard like a statue of one of those Greek thinkers and saying 'I wonder'. Then silence. Then 'I wonder'. Then silence.

Then suddenly words burst out of him.

'Now look, we know that Jesus tends to travel a lot so today could be our last chance. Obviously the front door is a non-starter. So is the back door – because there isn't one. A tunnel is out because we haven't a shovel. So it looks like the roof, lads. Let's find out where Jesus is talking, bind Simon to the stretcher with our belts, remove a bit of thatch, lower Simon in, and hey presto!'

Simon was drifting in and out of sleep and really in no mood to complain.

Put into practice

So we did it. Simon did wake up but seemed to accept what was going on and, in next to no time, part of the roof was stripped and he was lowered like a baby in a cradle. Well, the looks on those clustered round Jesus would have done credit to a goldfish convention. But Jesus just smiled and actually made sure that Simon had a safe landing, then stood back while a couple of us jumped down next to him. I had this little speech all prepared but fortunately did not have to give it. Mind you, it was a close thing because Jesus just said: 'Your sins are forgiven you'.

Well, at this, some of those around him started shuffling and muttering: 'Who does he think he is, God?'

I thought at first he meant our sins for stripping the roof. But he was looking at poor old Simon just lying there. To be fair to him, if he had not been feeling so ill, I reckon he would have been a bit disappointed. I know I was. After all the trouble we had gone to, and the expense – well, we'd have to repair the roof – just to have his sins forgiven was a bit of an anti-climax. Well, be honest. Put yourself in our shoes. What would you think?

A result

Anyway, before I could launch into my prepared speech about Simon's accident, Jesus said something to those standing near him that I did not catch and then to Simon: 'All right, pick up your stretcher and go home.' (At least, that is what was recorded in the *Capernaum Chronicle*. What he actually said, with a bit of a chuckle, was: 'Pick up your ladder and go home.' But I suppose the reported version has a better ring to it for posterity.)

So that was what Simon did, as natural as you like, as if there had been nothing wrong with him. It was as if he had been carrying the piece of ladder around with him all his life.

Well, how do you react?

The crowd reacted with a mixture of 'oohs' and 'ahs' and some fell to the ground as we all followed Simon out. Last in, first out.

I can vaguely remember myself going up to Jesus and saying something like: 'Thank you very much, sir. You don't know what it means to us. If there is anything I can do for you.'

Looking back on it, I suppose it was a silly thing to say to a Messiah. But you don't think of that at the time, do you? I mean, you just want to show you are grateful.

Still a team

Anyway that was yesterday. I did notice that Simon had slipped off quite early this morning. Immediately we got home, he talked about becoming a follower of Jesus. To be honest I just thought it was the euphoria of the moment, but it appears not. It's a pity really that our group is splitting up, but I suppose it was inevitable sometime. In a funny kind of way, I'm inclined to think that what we've been through together over the last few weeks will probably make us that much closer in the future, wherever we are. Funny that, isn't it?

Humanly ordinary

Just between the two of us, I seem to have put a few years' thinking into the last twenty-four hours. Well, you don't meet a Messiah everyday, do you? And, do you know, the thing that impressed me most was not the fact of him healing Simon? Obviously, that really was fantastic; but no. It was the way that, as Simon was about to come into land on his ladder, Jesus came forward and helped him in. Nobody else did; at least, not until they saw Jesus doing it. And then that smile. A good, honest one, not like those plastic ones people put on when they are doing public things. No. Just as if he meant it. Which I am sure he did. You don't meet that too often. I mean, don't get me wrong, I am not likely to leave everything I have here and go and follow him. That's not my scene. It wouldn't be all that responsible anyway, would it? Not with having Judith and the two youngsters. No, it's just that when something like that happens, you just can't let it wash over you, can you? It's like... Oh, you know what I'm trying to say, don't you?

A Blind Man Named Bart

*The miracle of the healing of blind Bartimaeus
Told by one of Bartimaeus' friends*[*]

Bartimaeus?

Well, we always called him Bart. In fact, come to think of it, it was only on a couple of occasions that it dawned on us that he might have another name. There was one evening when a group of better-off folk (not just better-off than us; that would be easy!) stepped over us on their way back from some festival or other. I reckon they had had a few goblets of the local brew as they were in a very jolly mood. This woman with a cracked-crystal voice chimed in: 'Oh, I say, surely that is Bartimaeus.'

He didn't look up. Well, it would have done no good, would it? What with him being blind and all. But I later got to thinking whether he would have recognised the voice. Anyway, that was one occasion and there was another one, though I forget when that was.

Closed in

Mind you, Bart was a strange one. Still is, I suppose. He hasn't always been blind, oh no, but none of us ever knew how it happened. We got the impression that whatever caused it had happened a long time before he joined us. I also have a suspicion that he had had a pretty good job as well. Don't ask me why; just one of those hunches. Possibly he was a doctor, maybe even a lawyer. But that is all guesswork because he didn't talk about himself much, or his family, if he ever had one. Well, he must have had one, but you know what I mean. It was as if the extent of

---

[*] This story can be found in Luke, chapter ten.

his vision was the extent of his life. And what went on inside that black horizon was a total mystery, at least to us. Now, don't get me wrong, he wasn't unsociable or anything. And he would help anybody. No, he was good like that. But as for personal stuff, you could forget it. He just didn't go there.

Social drinking

It's interesting, really, because most of us get a bit maudlin after we have a drink or three, but not Bart. No way. And he did take a drink like the best of us. But, thinking about it, I can't remember him getting completely legless or anything. I never saw him blind drunk, sorry about that.

In fact, to be honest, I have a sneaking suspicion that his loss of sight had something to do with drink; that something happened when he was in drink, and he now drank in such a way to show that, although it had bitten him, he was still in control. I may be wrong, but you just get these gut feelings every now and again, don't you? You see, that is me. I go a lot on gut feelings.

Moving on…

The other thing that did intrigue us as well was that he was always trying to improve himself. Now, as for me, Jake and Zach, we were quite contented with our lot. By and large we got enough food and if we didn't then we went hungry. The weather wasn't too bad; if it rained, we got wet; when it stopped, we got dry. But Bart, well, he was different; educated. Mind you, none of us knew exactly how clever he was. He used to quote from these books he'd read but, to be honest, we never knew what he was talking about. It was stuff in Greek and Latin. At least, that is what he said and who were we to argue?

…And then hanging around

And then he would go quiet for days. He'd just sit there, looking into space. Well, not exactly looking, but you know what I mean. We just put it down to his condition. Now, don't get me wrong, we all got on well together and Bart was very much part of us, but, although we were all different, he just seemed more different than the rest of us. Whether it was his educated background, the fact he was the only blind man among us, or what, I don't know.

For this?

But it all changed when this Jesus came along. When I say 'this Jesus', it might sound as if I am trying to put him down but I'm not. Honest. It's just that we'd never really seen him; just heard about him, kind of second-hand. We'd heard people discussing him as they passed by. Maybe they thought we were deaf, or maybe not there. We were invisible, especially when they were talking about what he did for poor people. You could tell that some of them were not all that keen on that. We had also heard about him healing people. And some even complained about that. I ask you! I remember one real know-all who insisted that if God rested on the sabbath so should Jesus; why should he be different from God? Can't say I knew exactly what he was talking about, but I have a suspicion Bart might have had a clue. As I say, he was real clever.

Anything is possible… isn't it?

Anywhere, where was I? Yes, only yesterday (it seems longer) we heard that Jesus was in the area and we got on to Bart, saying that at his age it could be his last chance and that he should go for it; get his eyes back. Well, he wasn't all that keen – he was in the middle of one his quiet periods. So Jake asked him straight out what would he say if Jesus came and said to him: 'Well Bartimaeus, my old friend, what would you like from me?'

Bart looked at Jake with those glazed eyes of his and said: 'Well, if he is who he says he is, he should know what I want, without asking. But, if he does ask me, I will say that I would like to smell better.'

At this, Nat said that he didn't think that Bart smelled all that bad anyway and we all laughed too loud because we had been drinking.

On the road

Anyway, when we had finally stopped laughing we heard this sound rolling towards us along the road. Yes, you've guessed it; it was Jesus and his friends, with quite a large crowd of people. The noise was coming from the questions he was being asked, the crowd members talking among themselves, and a few children who just liked the idea of making a noise. Nobody told Bart who it was. I suppose it was our fault, really. The number of times we used to point out things to him and then realise. I once saw someone stand up for a blind man on a large public transport cart assuming he would see the empty seat and sit down. He didn't and a cheeky little boy took the seat. Mind you, only for about three seconds – or was it two? But anyway, as I was saying, nobody told Bart but there was no need. We all stayed pretty quiet. Well, we had heard such a lot about Jesus but never seen him, so we put our effort into looking and watching closely as he was passing by.

Blind Bart speaks up

Then, as if a tap had been turned on at full pressure, Bart suddenly started to shout: 'Jesus, have pity on me!' Well, I can tell you it took us quite by surprise. And 'have pity'? What was he getting at? To be fair, we all thought that Bart had lost it. Well, you know, with the sun and the frustration and all that. You need to find some rational explanation for something so out of character. So we told him to keep quiet, but it did no good.

'Jesus, Son of David, have pity on me.' He even gave him his full title this time. We told him to keep quiet again and Jacob actually put his hand over his mouth, which was not a good idea because Bart bit him, so that tactic was suspended, though he didn't draw blood or anything.

Then the people close to Jesus took up our cry of 'Keep quiet'. A couple closest to Jesus started a bit of improvised coughing practice and one actually started whistling.

And Jesus responds

Suddenly the noise was shattered by silence; weird really. Then Jesus said, 'Where are you?' We toyed with asking Jesus if he was blind. I mean Bart, by this time, was standing up. He's a good six-footer and big with it, which made the scene all the stranger as he said, in a strong but polite voice, 'Please, have pity on me.'

Jesus made his way across to where the voice had come from. You know, I can still see those eyes: strong, piercing, nothing wimpish about that man. We pushed Bart forward. Actually, I stood up and led him forward because the ground was bit pot-holey and we didn't want to be asking for any more miracles. Jesus asked Bart what he could do for him. I waited for the smell comment or 'Do me a favour, Messiah' or something. But again, in a strong voice, not pleading, but almost suggesting it was his right: 'I would like to be able to see again, please.'

And Jesus looked at him. You could tell he was impressed. 'You believe I can do it, don't you?' Bart just nodded.

'And so I can. Your faith has saved you.'

Opening eyes

And Bart's eyes suddenly changed. Don't ask me how because I could no more explain it than I could fly; but they did. I mean they were open before but blind eyes are not really open, are they? He looked at me and started to blink quite furiously. And then he squinted through the slits. And slowly but surely the slits became larger until his eyes were fully open and he said: 'Thanks, Matt.' Then he turned back to Jesus and said: 'Thank you, sir.'

Well, I went back to the lads then. Jesus and his crowd moved off with Bart following behind them, walking and looking from side to side and jumping and skipping; a bit like the stump of a tail on the end of a dog.

A definite maybe

I've not seen Bart since. Mind you, it was only yesterday. You see I've got a bit of a problem, as well as my hangover (Well, we had to celebrate, even in Bart's absence). But listen, I don't need pity or anything like that. I can see and hear and walk and do all those things. There's just something nagging at me and I'm not quite sure what it is. I think it was when Bart used the word 'pity' and Jesus said later: 'You believe I can do it. And I can.' I just thought maybe he does other things besides eyes. Well, I know he does but you know what I mean. And I know he is not far away. In fact, the odds are he is only in the next village. But I am not sure I want to see him just yet. I mean, with Bart there was something definite: he was blind. But with me, I don't know. And, anyway, these are my friends, OK? As I said earlier, life is not brilliant but it is steady. I've got no real worries, no responsibilities, no nothing, really.

To leave this and... well, it would take a heck of a decision and I'm not quite sure. If he comes this way again, well, I'll maybe do something about it. Maybe. Mind you, until I'm certain I'm not looking into those eyes again.

A Good Year for Chianti

The marriage feast at Cana
Told by the Apostle Judas

An outsider

I often wondered if it was because I was from a different background: Mother owning 'Leaves "r" Us', that rather exclusive vegetarian restaurant on Temple Street, Father working in the City and me graduating with a 2:1 in Economics and Business Studies from the University of East Israel – or Damascus Poly as it was in those days – then joining Jacob & Sons on Solomon Way and living in Seaview Mews.

'Very nice,' I hear you say. Yes it was. That's what I gave up. Well, not exactly. The flat is still in my mother's name. You never know what the future holds, do you?

Kind of mixture

And, as you can imagine, all that is a long way from the fish-scaled banks of the Sea of Galilee. But don't get me wrong; I'm no snob. Sure, I went to a good school, but my parents had to scrimp and save. There I learned the value of money and hard work; proper standards. Most of the group are just, well, different. Quite a preponderance of what my mother calls 'ordinary working folk'. And I suppose she is right. They are fishermen and the like; artisans.

There are exceptions of course. Luke is a GP, often referred to as a physician, but, between you and me, I suspect that is more of an honorary title. And you often see pictures of Matthew sitting in his counting house, surrounded by piles of money but, believe me, he is no financier. To be honest, being a tax collector is little more than being on the check-out in a supermarket. And I know because Ruth, my ex-girlfriend, used to work at Goldstein's in Lidel Street. Only during the vacation, mind you. Now, don't get me wrong, Matthew and Luke are both nice men and not unintelligent. In fact, I did hear that Luke is writing a book about our group and the way we have developed. It should be good. Apparently, because of his position, being party to confidences and things, much of his information is from women. I personally think this is good, because women very often don't get the credit they deserve and they are good talkers.

The call

But, to be honest, I've not really been happy from the start. Initially, I was very flattered to be asked, or 'called' as people say nowadays. Always a bit of an ego boost, isn't it? The group themselves had a reputation for being a bit political with a cavalier attitude to some of our laws, particularly those to do with the sabbath and things. But I could live with that. The atmosphere at home when I was growing up had always been more *Guardian* than *Telegraph*... no, it was just... I don't know.

I suppose the first real challenge came after about six months. I had a ticket to see the Capernaum Crusaders (my team) play the Bethsaida Bulldogs the following night. It was the local derby. I had been a season-ticket holder once but, since I had joined the group, and especially since I had become the treasurer, I had not got to many games. So I was really looking forward to this one.

The challenge

And then suddenly, out of the blue, we were going to a wedding. Apparently, it was the daughter of some friends of Jesus' family. His mother and father had met these people years ago in Bethlehem round about the time he was born. They took them in when there was nowhere to stay or something. And they'd kind of kept in touch ever since.

'They are a nice couple, so I said we would go,' said Jesus.

'Wait a minute,' I said. 'We? Are you sure the invitation was for all of us?'

Now, whoever suggested silence was golden was not there

when my question got the lead balloon treatment. Actually, I knew there was no use making a fuss because we were doing most things together in those early days. It was what James used to refer to as 'team building'. I thought that was rich, coming from him, bearing in mind that he and his brother John only joined because their mother told them to.

Implications

The trouble was that, having accepted we were going, the others didn't seem to realise there were things to consider, like whether we would have to buy a present or not, how much we would have to pay for it, would we have to take anything like food or drink. You see, there was only really me who thought about things like that. But apparently it turned out there was no panic. We just had to take ourselves. It seemed that, although they were a fairly poor couple, they would just be glad for us to be there. I must admit, I would have thought that if they were poor the opposite would apply: they would need helping out. Just shows how people can have a different view of life. But anyway, I didn't push the point because, to be honest, we were a bit low on shekels.

Not at home

So we went. And it was obvious to me as soon as we walked in that they were not really expecting all of us. I still reckon, though I didn't make a big thing about it – bearing in mind what happened afterwards – that the invite was just for Jesus and his mother. Don't get me wrong, there were no snide comments or looks of surprise or anything. No, it was just that I could tell. We were shown into the main hall where the wedding was to be held. I remember feeling like a spare part, trying to make polite conversation about the weather and the price of olives. I used to be good at cocktail party small talk but it is amazing how quickly you lose the knack.

And do you know, although it is only about eighteen months ago, I can hardly remember a thing about the wedding itself? I do know that it seemed to go on for ever. There was loads of singing and chanting and things. Mind you, to be fair, that side of religion never did do much for me. Oh, I believe in God and all that and I can see so much sense in what Jesus says, but that is different.

To do with money

At the reception – it was a buffet – I got talking to a chap who worked for HSBC in Jerusalem. He was a nice man and very well connected; more my type, to be honest. He assured me if ever I wanted any advice on what he called 'creative accounting' that I was to get in touch. He even gave me his e-mail address. He seemed very sympathetic to my position: no guaranteed income, money given to the poor at a whim, limited assets and it all left to me to make sure we had enough to get by and to put something away for a 'dry day'. (Apparently in some countries people refer to a 'rainy day' which seems strange to us as we are always threatened by drought.)

Starting to happen

I was wondering how the football was getting on but there was no signal for my mobile in the hotel. I decided to try outside. That's when I saw Mary, Jesus' mother, talking to the bride's parents. I was fairly close but I don't think they saw me. The gist of it seemed to be that she was apologising for Jesus bringing along his friends – us.

I heard the girl's parents say, 'Don't be silly, Mary, it's been a great day. It's just if we'd realised, we'd have got more food in. And drink.' You see, I knew I was right.

Mary then turned to Jesus, who had just come up, and asked him if he had any ideas. He kind of gave a knowing look, like when people are accused of something and they say, 'What, me?' (This was a few months before the loaves and fishes incident so Jesus didn't have much of a track record at this time.)

I like Mary, you know. She's a fairly quiet lady; tends at times to be in her own little world, as if pondering things that had been said to her in the past, but she always had an eye out for others. You know, I always believe that it was thanks to her that Jesus went to see Lazarus that time he died. Maybe not; it's just a hunch.

Happening

Anyway, so there I am, standing behind this palm tree, thinking about the look that Jesus had given his mother, when – now listen to this – he called the servants across and they immediately began refilling the water jars to the brim. There were about six in all. Now, I don't know whether you have ever seen the jars they use but they are pretty big. Not quite as big as in the Ali Baba story but not far off. Anyway, he told one of the servants to fill a glass and take it to the man who was MC for the day. So he did. The man took a sip then screwed up his eyes and twitched his nose, a bit like that character in *Watership Down*. But despite the pantomime, I reckoned he knew his wines. He called the bridegroom across – I had got a bit closer by now – and said: 'Noah, this is brilliant. I've never tasted wine like it. Honest. It will be wasted on them in there, you know. I mean most of them wouldn't know their Rioja from their Ribena when sober, never mind when they've had their fill.'

I liked that phrase 'had their fill' – so much more refined than 'fluted'.

And then he used that famous phrase which you still hear used in various circumstances: 'You have saved the best wine till last.'

Now, the look on Noah's face was worth travelling to see. He gave a room-filling, beaming smile with a hint of 'I don't understand any of this' behind it. Well, once most people had had a few glasses or so of this new wine they seemed to forget there was a shortage of food as well. As my parents had always taught me the value of moderation, I didn't drink too much, though I did manage to decant some and take it home to my father and we both agreed it actually was a very pleasing Chianti classico.

Typical

The whole episode was typically Jesus. Obviously, he had arranged all this somehow, though nobody knew how. It wasn't magic or anything because I have seen that. That's all waving arms and wringing hands and moaning and groaning to any god who might be listening. No, this was nothing like that. Also it was typical Jesus that it was the best. As he used to say: 'Nothing is too good for other people.' Plus choosing Chianti, with its Italian connection, was definitely one in the eye for the Romans.

My future

And that's it really. It was a very strange incident. I suppose it really sticks in my mind because it was the first time I had seen Jesus really step outside the box. It was also, as I said, the first time I started to have second thoughts. I think it had something to do with the way the others looked at money. I don't mean just leaving it to me. No, that was my job. It was more the value they put on money and possessions and things. I'm not sure that is the way forward, though it's certainly different. But I will stick at it for a while until my mind is clearer. Hopefully I will get the courage to make an informed decision sometime. The group are big on forgiveness so there shouldn't be too much trouble if I decide to leave. And with what I have managed to save and my family's savings I should be all right. I hope so. I must admit that my eyes have been opened during my time with the group, but I am not sure it is for me in the long term. But then who knows what the future holds?

Judas Iscariot reputedly took his own life eighteen months after this account was written. Jesus of Nazareth was crucified a day later.

The Right Place at the Right Time

The feeding of the five thousand
Told by the young boy who provided the five loaves
and two fish*

The secret of success

I own a chain of bagel bars that spread from Jerusalem to Jericho. I also own Oxen's, one of the most exclusive salt beef restaurants in the whole of Israel. But I am not a proud man, oh no, I am prepared to give credit where it is due. And therefore I hold my hand up and say I owe much of my success to Jesus. Yes, that Jesus. Your Jesus. I learned from him the secret of success – being in the right place at the right time. I am an old man now and my story goes back a long way.

Presentation is everything

I suppose it really starts when I was about ten or eleven; too old for school and too young for retirement. Each day I used to go down to the market and buy fish, a few loaves of bread, a bit of fruit and the odd pickle and bitter herb. Then I would set off to whatever celebration or public gathering happened to be taking place and resell them. The profit margin wasn't great but you have to start somewhere. I mean, we don't know what Marks was doing before he met Spencer, do we? I started with one of those hand-held baskets. Boy, that was rough on the wrists! Then I graduated to a small handcart. It was always spotless; you could see your face in the paintwork and the shiny bits glistened. I had two 'whiter than white' cloths – one underneath the food, the other to keep the flies off – and a lid that kept everything (apart

---

* This story can be found in John, chapter six.

from me) fairly cool. My grandfather Solomon always used to tell me that presentation was everything. He was a wise old man and he was right. I also had two shirts: one for travelling and one for selling. Clean boy, clean food. I did quite well.

The newcomer

But the real breakthrough came one weekday morning. To say it was a warm day is to say nothing for that year; we were having one of the best summers in thirty years, and that was the best since records began. Now, I had heard that this man Jesus was preaching up on the hill. He was the new kid on the block, really making a name for himself. He was very much his own man; no agent or anything. Not popular with everyone, but that's life, eh? The publicity had suggested that he was due to be making some pretty startling revelations. So I thought, Jacob, my boy, that is where you need to be. Hungry ears mean hungry mouths.

And, as my reputation for good quality food was slowly building up, I was quite excited. I had decided to buy double the amount of stuff I normally did. It was a bit of a risk, but, even in those early days, I was learning the value of sensible speculation.

Well, you should have seen the crowds. I can still remember it as if it was yesterday. It made the annual Passover sales at Harrods look like a meeting in a telephone box. In fact I heard one old man mutter through his grey straggly beard that he had never seen anything like it since the public executions of years earlier. I took his word for it.

A preacher of note

Anyway, there I was, working the crowds, pulling my medium-sized smooth-running handcart and doing quite a brisk trade. And then, for no apparent reason, things suddenly ground to a halt. It was a bit like the M13 from Jerusalem to Samaria on a Thursday evening.

Well, I was a bit tired anyway so I decided to have a sit down. As it happened, I wasn't far from the top of the hill that Jesus was speaking from. He was in full flow by this time, arms waving and all that, dropping his voice and then slowly getting louder – all the tricks. Even young as I was in those days, I could see he was really into what he was saying. Anyway, there I was listening and, to be honest, I got quite interested. He was using examples I could relate to, like the importance of dough in a batch of bread and pulling donkeys out of ditches. (Well, I mean, I had had to do that myself on more than one occasion. Not with a donkey, but with my cart.)

Then suddenly it all went quiet. The people waited, a bit fidgety, but nobody moved. Jesus seemed to be having some kind of discussion with his followers. A little bit heated as well. I don't mean screaming and shouting and throwing things, but shall we say a 'civilised disagreement'. I had more or less decided that it was time to move on myself when it happened…

Lending food

One of Jesus' friends – I was going to say henchmen but he was not that kind of man – came across to me, pointed at my handcart and said: 'Hey, you, son. Have you any food left?' (Business is business so I did not insist on the courtesy of 'please'.) I let him have a look. There were a few bits of bread and a couple of quite small fish. Now, it is normally a buyer's market but I had a clue I might be on to a winner here, so was prepared to bump the price up a bit. You can imagine my surprise when the man – whom I reckoned knew a bit about fish – said: 'Will you just lend me a couple of those for a few minutes?'

'Lend?' Now I had heard some things in my short life but to lend fish and bread? And you will never believe this – especially if you know me now – but I actually said: 'Yes, of course. Help yourself,' because I was so gobsmacked. I also offered to lend him a bitter herb and a pickled onion but he didn't seem to hear me. He took the bread and fish and handed them over to Jesus.

Generous mystery

Now, what happened next is still a blur. In fact, even then I was not fully sure what was going on. All I do know is that suddenly food started to appear from all over the place. People who had been sitting on their hands looking miserable, hungry and shifty, suddenly had a couple of fish – and good quality, too – in each hand and some nice crusty bread. Others had the odd bit of quiche and pizza slices, but they were in the minority. Others did not seem so lucky, but it was nice to see people sharing stuff about. And then – and you are not going to believe this – someone next to me offered me a lovely pickled herring and a bagel to eat. It was very fresh with quite a specific taste. Never found to this day where he got it from. It wasn't one of mine. And now listen to this – the man who borrowed the food came back to me and gave me seven fish and twice as much bread as I had given him. I actually shared it with those around me. Well, you do, don't you? I mean, business is business but there is a limit. And even in those days I was learning the value of public relations and loss leaders and things like that.

The in-crowd

Over the next year or so, I followed Jesus and his friends around. I actually got to know a couple of them quite well. There was one of them called Thomas. I remember having a chat with him and him telling me that, when they borrowed the food from me, he wasn't sure what it was all about. He said it had been a real jump of faith for him to go along with Jesus on that occasion. And there were others. Peter (the Apostle formerly known as Simon), John, Nathaniel and Judas. Now he was an interesting case. Always drove a hard bargain that one, but I could respect that. Yet there was another side to him that I could not work out. Of course, he hanged himself, you know, so he really must have been going through something. Pity really because he never seemed to show it. Just proves it is not a good thing to judge by appearances.

Strictly business

You know, when I look back on those early days, anybody might think I had become a follower. But, let me tell you, it was strictly business. I must admit I found what Jesus was saying was good but it was not for me. No. I kind of became their official outside caterer. I actually toyed with putting on my barrow 'by appointment to the future Messiah,' but as he was not all that popular with the authorities I decided it might not be a good idea. They used to let me know when there was to be an extra large gathering.

Of course, I used to give a discount. I got to know all the catchphrases, especially that one about love your neighbour and you will be OK. That used to come up time and time again in different forms. I was also there on that day he cleared the Temple of those people who had set up stalls there. I suppose I shouldn't have been, but I was particularly glad of that because I had once applied for a franchise there and had been turned down for no good reason that I could see. Glad I didn't get it now.

The last time

The last time I saw Jesus was quite a sad affair and I still feel a little bit guilty at being there. I suppose I was about thirteen. In those days, every now and again they would have public crucifixions. The procession would start in town and go up to Golgotha. Now, they always drew a good crowd. Even folk who could not be there on the hill would take a few minutes out of work to watch the procession pass by. So I set up my stall. Oh yes, I had graduated to a stall by now. Funny really, when I look back, because it was Jesus who gave me a couple of tips on how to make it solid yet still portable, with the right joints and stress bars. Apparently, his dad had been a carpenter. Anyway, there I was on the corner of Main Street and Gethsemane Way. Experience had taught me that the best trade was before the procession arrived. Then there was a lull as people watched. So you can imagine my surprise when I recognised the cross-carrier as Jesus.

Not right

I remember feeling then that this could not be happening. What wrong had he done? OK, I knew he had criticized the authorities and that, but surely the priests and leaders of the people could not be so small-minded and vindictive? It seemed they could. The procession passed, I dismantled my stall and I followed, all the way. And I saw him die. Yes, I did. Fortunately there were a few people – I counted five – with him when he died. But where were the others? I got to thinking about the many people he had healed and helped and encouraged. And, of course, I thought of the few thousand who had benefited from the time my food was lent to him. People have short memories, don't they? Or maybe 'selective memories' is a better phrase.

An influence

And that is my story. That tight-knit little group seemed to vanish after that. Well, maybe not vanish but just took a different direction. No more big meetings or anything like that. As a group they are still not very popular, even today. But I must admit I have never found them a problem. Obviously, some of the things Jesus said and did must have rubbed off on them. And, to be honest, he had quite and effect on me too, though I would not like that to get to be public knowledge, what with my position in the community and all that. You know what I mean?

The Cohens at Number 8

The raising of Lazarus
Told by one of the neighbours in the street[*]

Our street

Methuselah Avenue is a nice place to live, full of old traditional houses. Most of the residents have been there, like me, for the best part of thirty years. The Cohens at Number 8 have probably been around the longest, three generations to my knowledge. Old Granny Cohen seemed to have lived there for ever. In fact, Abe Bloom at Number 6, a real comedian, once spread a rumour that she was one of Moses' first girlfriends. And when my youngest, Sara, asked her if this was true, Granny Cohen denied it with a sufficient lack of conviction to add to the confusion in the child's mind.

She died some time ago. If she'd have hung on for a few more years, she would have buried both her son and daughter-in-law. It was a tragedy that, both getting TB within a couple of years of each other, leaving just the three children, Martha, Mary and Lazarus as orphans. And, even though she was only in her mid-teens, Martha smoothly took on the role of mother and was absolutely brilliant. Lazarus was the baby of the family and thoroughly spoilt by his two elder sisters.

Mary, although she was a lovely child and only a couple of years younger than Martha, was a bit of a dreamer. She got religion early and every now and again would vanish for a few months and then suddenly return home as if nothing had happened. It turned out that she used to follow various religious movements and leaders of the time. That's one thing about our country: it's never short of a messiah or two doing the rounds.

---

[*] This story can be found in John, chapter eleven.

Coincidence or not?

The latest messiah to come on the scene, of course, is Jesus. He's a friend of the Cohens and that's how I got to know him. And listen to this – apparently, Jesus' mother had met Mrs Cohen at a Bible summer school a couple of years before Jesus was born. They became good friends and visited each other now and again until they each had their first children, Jesus and Martha, about the same time. After that, they wrote to each other. And then, when young Mary Cohen was talking to Jesus after one of his meetings the connections were made. It was a real coincidence. In fact, I once said this to Jesus and, although he agreed very politely, I did get the impression that he didn't do coincidences.

A social Messiah

I think he used the Cohen's house as a bit of a bolt-hole really. Not too far from Jerusalem, where it was all happening, yet far enough away. It was ideal, because, when you think about it, it must be quite difficult being the Messiah: hardly any time to yourself; always on call; and it's not as if you can have a day off, is it, and let someone else tell the parables and work the miracles? Must be a tough job, I reckon. So it was good that he became very much part of our group.

You see, living in a cul-de-sac, by and large we get on well with each other. So your friends are my friends. And we have the odd social event, like barbecues – with selected meats, of course. Jesus was always welcome, especially as he usually brought a really good bottle of wine. No label or anything, but real genuine good stuff. Not sure where he got it from, but it was much appreciated.

I also went for a drink with him and Lazarus on a couple of occasions. He wasn't a heavy drinker – the odd half-litre of Budweiser. I actually think it did him good. He was a nice man, very open to new ideas and he had a good sense of humour, kind of dry, more subtle than belly laugh, if you know what I mean. I remember him telling a couple of wicked Pharisee jokes; gentle, but with a point. Yes, he became very much part of us in Methuselah Avenue.

Absent friends

And that is really what made it all very strange when suddenly Lazarus got quite ill. Now, to be honest, he was not a well man at the best of times. He always appeared to have a permanent cough or sniffle. But this time it seemed a bit worse. Unconfirmed reports did suggest that Martha and Mary had tried to get word to Jesus. I myself thought it was just to inform him; after all, they were really close friends. But some of the others had different ideas. You see, by this time he had built up quite a reputation for being a healer and a multiplier of bread and a maker of wine. So Toby from Number 10 suggested he might have come and done something. In his words: 'I mean what is the use of having a messiah for a friend if you can't make use of him.' Now this might seem a bit cruel and even coarse but you have to remember where Toby was coming from. His son owned Omega Cars, 'The Last Word in Motors' in Jerusalem, so there was always a new vehicle on his drive. They were salesmen through and through.

All very sudden

Anyway, to get to the point, one Friday on my way to work – I was on a double shift that day at the brewery – I noticed that the Cohens' curtains were drawn. I thought nothing of it, but when I came back they were still drawn and my wife told me it was Lazarus. He had died. Yes, died. Well, I can tell you I was shocked. I mean, it's a fact, isn't it, that people who are always ill never die? It is always those who look after them. But it was true. And not only dead but he was already in his tomb. Mind you, that's our tradition, as you know, all done and dusted by sunset, especially with the next day being the sabbath and all. I went across, of course, to give my condolences. Martha was busying herself making tea and baking bread and serving people. Mary was in a heap in front of the fire. I didn't stay too long – well, you don't, do you? Just long enough to find out that Lazarus had had a bit of a fever and the tablets he got from the doctor had kind of reacted with him. It was never said but I knew the girls were thinking, 'Here we go again' as visions of the way their parents had died were there in their minds.

In his time

And there was also a sense of 'Where is Jesus?' in the air. Now, don't get me wrong, they were not making a big thing about it. In fact, looking back on it, I am not sure they actually said anything at all. It was just a feeling I got; I sometimes do, you know. My wife says it is a gift.

Well, the next couple of days were a blur, but I do remember a few days later, on a Monday morning, I was in the front garden tying up the fence, which I reckoned had been leant on too heavily by party-goers the night before. I looked up the street and there, approaching, was Jesus and some of his friends. I don't know what it was, maybe the sun behind him and the long shadows in front, maybe that long dusty cloak thing he used to wear, or something, but it just looked like an opening scene from one of those spaghetti westerns when the man with no name walks into town to do good. As Jesus was going to do. Anyway, before I had chance to ask him how he was, he went into the Cohen's. I later learned he had already met Martha and Mary on the outskirts of town. Martha had come back to get something for him and his friends to eat. Mary stayed with him. Anyway, they all went into the house and the door was closed.

Plain talking

And then, before you could say anything, they all came outside again. They definitely hadn't had time for a cup of tea, though maybe they had an eye on the celebrations that would follow. They walked back up Lebanon Road and turned left into Cedar Avenue. That's where most of the tombs are. I must admit they did look a sorry bunch. There was a real cloud of sadness around them. They were walking quite slowly; in fact, so slowly that, without realising it, I almost caught them up. To be fair, they wouldn't have minded because, as I say, we all get on well in our cul-de-sac. Mary was in a right old state, looking as though she was not sure whether to sob or weep. Martha was obviously upset but holding it together more. Also, she had a face full of question marks. I heard her saying something like 'Yes, Jay' (her pet name for Jesus), 'of course I believe. I am surprised you need to ask me that knowing what we have been through. And, yes, I know he will rise again. But, to be honest, I was thinking later rather than sooner.'

Jesus made no response but you could see that what Martha had said had got to him.

Place of death

Anyway, we got to the tomb. It had Number 13 on the front in bright yellow letters (I must ask them about that, because all the other numbers were in black or purple). Jesus then turned to two of his friends, big burly ex-fishermen, and asked them to roll the stone from in front of the tomb.

Well, at this, most of the crowd, and there was a fair-sized one by now, took a polite couple of steps back, pretending it was to give the family some privacy, but everybody knew it was to get as far away as possible from the expected body odour of Lazarus.

It was Martha who really summed it up. 'You are joking, aren't you, Jay? I mean he's been dead for about four days now. The aroma could be sharp.'

What a phrase, eh? 'The aroma could be sharp.' You know, looking back on all this, I am quite surprised at myself. I'm normally very conscious of other people's space and privacy but here I was within earshot of everything that was being said. Mind you, to be fair, it was not a bad thing because the girls, Martha and Mary, were in such a state that they probably would not have remembered anything. But I actually did hear Jesus say: 'Now look here, Marty, we both know that I have gained a reputation for doing some pretty challenging things. And we both know it is not me who does them but rather the God we both accept. That is why I am doing it this way. For all to see. And not just in a private session.'

When Martha nodded she also said, not unkindly, 'OK Jay. That's cool. Do it your way.'

Place of life

Well, Jesus suddenly shouted out in a loud voice: 'Lazarus! Come out.' He put the fear of God into me, I can tell you, so I was not totally surprised at what followed. Now, for those of you who have read the various draft copies of this incident, you will know what happened next. All I want to say is that I was there and some of the exaggerations do nobody any favours; least of all Lazarus, or Jesus. First of all, the 'aroma' wasn't all that 'sharp'. Maybe a shower would have been in order later, but nothing like what you get from some of those farm lorries on the road to Bethany. Lazarus came out wrapped in bandages and things and walking a bit stiffly, but I suppose that is understandable. And then Jesus said, a lot more quietly: 'Untie him'. Two of his friends did just that. Jesus just stood there with his arms round the shoulders of Martha and Mary.

And that was it really. Once untied, Lazarus came across and hugged his two sisters and very shyly said to Jesus: 'Thank you, Jay.' One of the tabloids has suggested that his first words were 'I am dying for a drink' but I can tell you that that was just newspaper talk. He was so glad to be back with his family that I am sure food and drink and anything else was far from his mind. And then they all turned round and went back home through the parted crowds. No cheering. No 'Well I never' or anything like that. There was more of a stunned silence than anything else.

Sharing your barbecue

I suppose, really, it took couple of days for people to come to terms with it. Then the discussions started. Some suggested that this proved that Jesus was for real. Others felt that maybe it had been a trick. They questioned whether Lazarus had been ill enough to die and also pointed out that nobody had been guarding the tomb or anything. Somebody made the comment that he felt dying once was enough without having to go through it all again. But that was mainly outsiders. Us in the cul-de-sac more or less kept things to ourselves. We were happy for Martha and Mary, and for Lazarus. But it had not really sunk in that this actually happened here. It's like lottery winners and things. It's always someone somewhere else. But, I tell you, actually having someone like Jesus sharing our barbecue now would really take some getting used to.

First Come, First Served at the Sheep Pool

The healing of the man at the sheep pool
Told by a casual observer[*]

My wife

You see, my wife is not a well woman. But, worse than that, her mother lives with us. And she says it's my fault, as if I am to blame for the lack of rain for the last three years. So anyway, because of this, every afternoon for the last month or so, once I have got my wife settled, I've gone out for a bit of a walk.

The pool

And because I am not one of those people who can just walk for the sake of it, or just go round in circles goldfish-style, I decided to explore the city; Jerusalem, my newly-adopted city. Now, I know it is not enormous like London or Manchester but you'd be amazed how many miles you can walk when you are permanently lost. I tried the market but as soon as I got there people tried to sell me things – which I suppose is understandable. I walked round the city walls and then to each of the gates and back, which was pretty boring. Then, one day, quite by chance, I came across this pool of water – which, in a drought was not bad.

Just being there

But this was not any old pool. Oh no. It had five ornate arches around it, as if guarding it. And in the shade they threw was a whole army of sick people. And I mean sick, really sick, not many

---
[*] This story can be found in John, chapter five.

rashes and sniffles there. The smell was a bit rich as well, but that was OK because I don't mind smells. Now, if we talk taste, like hot curries or lumpy off milk, then that is a different story; but smells I can handle. Anyway, I was fascinated by the whole area and by the people there. Not in a kind of voyeuristic way like one of those documentaries on Channel 5, I mean serious fascination. Sensitive fascination, if you see what I mean. It was incredible. I just couldn't work it out. To start with, I kind of stood at the back, as you do, pretending that I wasn't really looking, remembering what my mother told me about it being rude to stare.

Only one winner

And then I went back the following day. It was then that someone suddenly started shouting 'It's moving' and there was a mad dash for the pool. Four people jumped in, two dived in and another one simply tripped and fell in. It looked like a dead heat to me who hit the water first but apparently that was not possible. There could only be one winner. They all started to crawl out of the water and go back to their places.

Apart from, that is, one oldish man who very slowly moved through the crowd with a saucer-sized grin. You could see he didn't want to appear too excited, but the effort proved too much and, without warning, he started to jump up and down and whoop and scream and yell: 'I have been cured! Praise the Lord!' And then he ran through one of the arches, which had 'Exit' above it. Well, to be honest, I couldn't tell what he'd been cured of because I didn't know what he had before and he ran away too quickly for me to ask him. The whole incident intrigued me even more, especially when you looked more closely at the water. Not exactly healthy-looking itself. Mind you, as we all know, appearances can be deceptive.

Habit forming

Anyway, after that, it became my daily routine: a walk to the pool. And, being a man of habit, I found myself always going through the same entrance and more or less sitting in the same spot, near one of those overflowing litter bins in which there was a variety of used bandages, elastoplasts and things, with flies buzzing around. Although I still felt a bit of a stranger, I also felt fairly safe. I always carried a book and wore heavy black plastic sunglasses; the 'see without being seen' type. But things soon changed.

A challenge

After the first week, this man turned to me and said: 'What's wrong with you, then?' I refrained from suggesting that as this was a free country I wasn't aware there was something wrong in being normal. And, to be honest, being a perfectly normal person, as I am, I was a bit challenged that this stranger should suggest I had any weakness or ailment. Mind you, I did wonder if he could see something in me I was not aware of. You never know. Some people have strange gifts. Anyway, I played safe – as normal people do – and said: 'Actually, I am all right, thanks very much, but my wife could be better.'

'Is she a big woman, then?'

I wondered where on earth that comment came from. Because, as it happens, by no stretch of the imagination could my wife be called big. I mean, she is not even small. She is smaller than that. Only on a really sunny day does she throw a shadow. But that is all to do with her illness. So I said 'Not really', to which my new-found conversationalist countered with: 'Well, why don't you bring her here? This is the place for cures, especially with you to help her.'

'Pardon me?' I said, in a tone of voice which I hoped would suggest honest curiosity without appearing patronising.

Acceptance

You see, although my wife was an invalid, she really wasn't in the same league as this man with his ragged clothing and slightly deformed legs and not too neighbour-friendly body odour. However, my non-committal approach was shattered by him saying 'Come and sit down here, son. My name is Simon. What's yours?'

I said it was Saul and I did as I was told. Well, not exactly *told*, although, thinking about it, yes, maybe 'told' was the right word.

It's amazing how being accepted by someone can be so persuasive. He drew me into his emotional embrace.

The secret of the pool

'Do you know where you are, lad?'

Now, geography has never been my strong point and I felt 'Yes, here' might be too flippant. So I said: 'How do you mean?' I hoped it would show genuine interest.

'You see that water down there?'

I said that I did.

'Well, every time it moves – and I mean moves,' he said, trying to jab me with his finger, but I was out of range, 'well then, the first person in gets a cure.'

Phrases like 'You must be joking', 'Pull the other one' and 'Do me a favour' lined up behind my front teeth but stood aside to allow 'What do you mean?' to escape first.

'Well, it is like this, son,' he continued in his avuncular way (yes I know with 'avuncular' he should have called me 'nephew' but let us not split hairs. Nobody says 'Well, it is like this, nephew, do they?) Anyway, as I was saying, he continued: 'This is a special pool, see. It goes back to our ancestors. And they say that when the "Angel of the Lord" – a technical phrase, my friend –' he winked in a conspiratorial way, like Fagin to Oliver, 'moves over the water, the first person to get into the pool gets cured.'

Handicaps

'I saw you standing back there last Wednesday when Thomas was healed. Now he had a really bad stomach. And what a smell! Much worse than me.' This time he winked with the other eye.

'Oh,' I said.

'But that's the trouble,' he went on. 'Just think about it. You see, stomachs and necks and arms have a good chance. Most internal problems, likewise; deaf people too, if they really concentrate; blind people, if pointed in the right direction. But me, a cripple, or Nick over there, with no legs at all... Well, we have no chance.'

'But that is not fair,' I said. 'Surely that proves this pool might be special but it isn't a God thing? I mean, you need a level playing field. It's not fair.'

'Well, who said life was fair, brother?' he replied.

Fair or not?

Then, as if on cue, these three fairly healthy-looking men, one of whom smelled faintly of fish, appeared through the entrance behind us. A whisper of 'That's him' could be heard. Anyway 'him' and his friends were suddenly standing above me and Simon, and very pleasingly keeping the sun off us both. 'Him' looked straight at me. Now, I don't know whether you have ever experienced this, but some people, and it is a real gift I reckon, could tell you your house had burned down, your pet cat had been barbecued and the insurance was out of date and you would still say 'thank you'. Well it was a bit like that.

'I heard you say it isn't fair. What do you mean by that?' he asked.

Well, I was all thumbs and consonants, but I had a go. Words tumbled out like 'Who is to blame for illnesses?' and 'I thought God had no favourites?' and 'What about the parents?' and 'Why did it always seem to happen to poor people?' Stuff like that. To be honest, I'm not sure what I said.

But he just replied, and not with any nasty or 'I am cleverer than you, so listen' attitude, 'Surely it is better that some rather than none get healed.'

I was going to say about one-legged blind people not having a chance but realised that he wasn't just referring to that. Then, talk about a surprise, he turned to Simon and asked him how long he had been disabled. Simon said he'd only been coming here a few years but he had actually been ill for over thirty-seven years. I did some quick mental arithmetic – because I was good at that at school but could never do algebra – and worked out that that must have been most of his life.

Obvious or not

Now, listen to this. This man, who it turned out was the hinted-at Messiah, Jesus, said: 'Do you want to get well?'

It seemed a daft question really but maybe not. Simon's reply was strange in the light of what was to happen: 'You are kidding! Have you ever seen a cripple out-sprint a man with a stomach ache?'

The odd thing about it is that it was not said in any sarcastic way. It was quite funny, really. Then Jesus simply said he was not talking about jumping into this pool – or any other pool come to think of it. 'There is more than one way to skin a cat,' Jesus said. Then, very calmly, he asked Simon to pick up his mat – I suppose 'that bit of rag you are sitting on' might have smacked of snobbery – and walk. And he did. No whooping. No praise the Lord-ing or anything like that. Just a simple 'Thank you, sir' and he walked away. And as everybody watched him go, he turned round and said to those he had become friends with, 'I'll be back'.

So sad

And we all watched him go, during which time Jesus and his friends quietly drifted away. I later discovered that some of the leaders had complained they had heard he had been curing people outside office hours; or 'on the sabbath' as they put it. Isn't it sad when people get so wrapped up in laws?

Open to options

I went home to my wife and on the way had a good think. It had been quite a day, giving me real food for thought. You know, looking back, one thing I was impressed by was that once Simon had been cured there was no kind of jealousy from anybody else. Also, nobody asked, which I would have thought they might have done, why he had cured just one and not all of them. It was strange, really; very strange. But, like Simon, I will be back. But next time I think I will bring the wife as well. It will give her a respite from her mother, if nothing else. I'm not really talking about a cure, not at this stage anyway.

I also feel I would like to get to know those people around the pool a bit better, maybe help them a bit. Not sure how, but definitely not just by pushing them into the water, maybe just by being there. It will be good to meet Simon again and see how he is getting on. Healing can be a funny thing. I must say, I was impressed by Jesus, even though I only met him for those few minutes. As for what he said to Simon – there is more than one way to skin a cat – I wonder if he made that up just for that occasion.

Please Call Me Thomas

An appreciation of Thomas the Apostle
Told by the various people who knew him throughout
his life[*]

Thomas, called the Twin, who was one of the Twelve, was not with them when Jesus came. When the disciples said 'We have seen the Lord', he answered 'Unless I see the holes that the nails made in his hands and can put my finger into the holes they made, and unless I can put my hand into his side, I refuse to believe.'

Eight days later, the disciples were in the house again and Thomas was with them. The doors were closed, but Jesus came in and stood among them. 'Peace be with you,' he said. Then he spoke to Thomas: 'Put your finger here; look, here are my hands. Give me your hand; put it into my side. Doubt no longer but believe.'

Thomas replied: 'My Lord and my God!'

Introduction

Although by no means one of the senior members of the College of Apostles, Thomas is an important member in the development of the early Church. Though chiefly known for his 'unless I can see with my own eyes' comment, there is so much more to the man than this. In the following pages we hope to show this by getting accounts from various people who knew Thomas at different stages of his life. We are aware that this might appear to smack of electioneering in the light of the newly-created Diocese of Bethsaida. This is not the case. As you know, we are a church, not a political party, and therefore have never gone in for such things. Some people are already saying that there is no white smoke without fire but I can honestly assure you that that is

---
[*] The story of Thomas can be found in John, chapter twenty.

merely a slick comment with no foundation in fact.
Happy reading. Bless.
Brian Levy (Editor, *Thomas: A Future Bishop without Doubt?*)

Interview A: Thomas

Thomas was the second child of John and Mary Rosen. In actual fact, he was a twin, but his sister Teresa died when only a few weeks old. He was born in a small village just outside Bethsaida. He went to the local village primary school and then moved on to Bethsaida Community College and later to the City University of Mid-Israel (formerly Jerusalem Poly). He married early. His wife, Miriam, died in a riding accident on the road to Damascus. As this book goes to print, Thomas is the parish priest of St Gabriel's in Tiberias.

I am pleased to write these few words in appreciation of myself. Jesus always used to tell us that if we did not love ourselves, how could we love others or even expect others to love us. I have found that very true throughout my life.

I am also pleased to put the record straight regarding the incident which *The Sun* notoriously described as the 'Holes in the Hand Scandal'. If you care to read the incident again, you will see that, in fact, I was not denying that Jesus had actually risen from the dead, but rather that I was not fully convinced by the accounts given by my fellow Apostles. In retrospect, that is possibly worse; but that was the case. Things were not as cut and dried in those days as have been portrayed.

Take, for example, that unfortunate business with Judas. As you have probably read, he took his own life, allegedly. Well, that left quite a hole in our organisation. Who would look after the money? Who would deal with the basic essentials of community living? Now, as I had been a family man – prior to my wife's riding accident – and treasurer of the Jew Soc at university, to a certain extent I was the obvious choice. Not that I minded. But it was not a completely smooth transition. There were problems. For the first few days in that room we existed solely on takeaways – conveniently delivered to the house as we were within a three-mile radius.

That was obviously not satisfactory. And, anyway, we needed a few basic necessities like toilet rolls and beer. So that's where I was on that fateful day; at Sainsbury's. So imagine my surprise when I returned be greeted by this frenzied revelation: Jesus has risen, honest! Well, it was a bit too much to take in immediately.

You see, look at it from my point of view. The atmosphere in that room was something else. The windows were locked and, with Nathaniel being a dedicated pipe smoker, it would have been easier to find a ghost in a fog. Also, I was aware that what with the lack of fresh air and fresh vegetables, the blood sugar of many of my friends would be a bit low. Many of them were sleeping a lot. So that was one thing to bear in mind. Also, some of them were into prayer big time. Then there was John. Even in those early days, he was prone to the odd dream and vision. So you see, I was just a little worried that some of them had possibly seen what they wanted to see and not what actually happened. And, to my mind, it was too important a thing to mess with.

It might seem as if I am trying to justify my attitude and maybe I am. But, you see, I deal in facts. Like when Peter walked on the water and then sunk when the wind got up. I always felt that that was a lack of forward planning on his part. How far away was Jesus? How deep was the water? What were the prevailing winds? These were the questions I felt he should have been asking. But that is me; I like to know where I stand. Commitment is so important, but I can't change my background. And I suppose it takes all kinds. I hope so.

Interview B: Sarah

Sarah was Thomas' older sister by four years. In reality, she really brought Thomas up after their father left home. This was the same time, as it happens, that Mrs Jordan from Number 11 also vanished, though nothing was ever proved. Their mum worked in the Bethsaida 24-hour Co-op on the corner of Jericho Avenue.

I remember them being born, you know; the twins, I mean. I was about four at the time. Things had been funny for some time in our house. My dad was constantly asking Mum if she was all right. And she was saying 'yes' through a mouthful of sardine and honey sandwiches. And all the time she was getting bigger and bigger. I had to sit on my dad's knee, which wasn't as comfortable; all edges and corners. Then, suddenly, Mum was thinner again. In those days, I presumed it was to do with no longer eating sardine and honey sandwiches. It was only later I found out the real reason. Although I had always wanted a puppy, who I decided I would call Rex, instead I got two babies called Thomas and Teresa.

Sadly, little Teresa died before we had chance to get to know her. And then – maybe I am imagining this – Mum and Dad seemed to change. I seem to remember them insisting that we should take nothing for granted, not even life. One of Dad's favourite sayings was: 'If in doubt, doubt.' I never fully understood what he meant then, but it has become clearer since. And that's how we were brought up. And then Dad left home and he never came back. I thought it was probably my fault because I only got a D in geography in my first year at Bethsaida Community College, but later on I dismissed that idea. When you think about it, it was so silly. Anyway, whatever reasons, I more or less had the job of bringing up our Tom, as mum had to work longer hours at the Co-op. But I enjoyed it. It gave me a good excuse to stay in because I didn't have many friends.

Thomas was a funny lad; so organised, even from a very early age. Everything had to be just right. I remember once we were going for a walk and it was pretty horrible weather so I got his anorak and wellington boots out. He was about six at the time. 'What they for?' he said. He used language as if the words cost.

I explained that it was going to rain and that was why.

'But not raining.'

No,' I explained, 'not raining but going to.'

'How you know?'

Well, instead of going into a long detailed explanation about clouds and winds and precipitation and all that, I simply said that the woman on the telly had said it would rain and that was good enough for me. But it wasn't good enough for him. He hadn't seen the woman on the telly. So he went out in his little trainers and carried his wellington boots. When it started to rain, he changed. And he got wet and fell over as he balanced on one leg under one of those Perspex see-through bus shelters with no seats, which were popular back in those days. But it didn't bother him. He was that kind of child: lovely, but stubborn.

And, to be honest, although he drove me round the bend in those early days, I wouldn't have swapped him for anything – well maybe a three-foot plasma TV. I'm joking.

Am I surprised he has got where he has? That he's nearly a bishop and all? Not really. I mean, I am not a follower myself but I reckon that it was the authority and confidence of that Messiah that finally won him over. He doesn't do wishy-washy, our Tom. He likes to know where he stands.

Interview C: Jacob, Thomas' best friend from junior school

Jacob lived in the same street as Thomas. As his sister, Zoë, was fifteen years older than him, Jacob was treated very much as an only child at home. Because of this he was quite self-contained and contented with life. In a way he was a strange choice of friend for Thomas.

First of all, I would like to say I am pleased to be asked to contribute to this small work about my friend, Tom. I feel that I can call him 'Tom' as he himself seems comfortable with the name now. But it was not always the case, you know.

I remember when we were both about eight years old, that name thing was quite an issue. Our teacher, Mrs Shameel, used to start each day with a short prayer. Then, once we had all sat down, she would say: 'Well, children, have we anything to share?'

Usually it was about cats having kittens or mothers having babies, but, this day, Tom suddenly piped up with: 'Yes, Mrs Shameel, I would like to let it be known to "hall and Sunday" that from today my name shall be Thomas.'

Well, the silence was deafening. But then it gave birth to a few sniggers and would possibly have grown into serious disruption if Mrs Shameel had not stepped in and said, in a loud clear solemn voice: 'Thank you, Thomas, for sharing that with us. Your wishes will be respected by all of us but please remember it is something new and mistakes will be made, so try not to take them to heart.'

To which he answered: 'I will try my best, Miss.'

'Now,' she said, 'would anybody else like to add anything to what Tom, sorry, Thomas, has just shared with us?' Silence again. So that was it. Thomas he wanted, so Thomas he was.

He did explain later his reason for changing back to his birth name. He felt that names with two syllables sounded more dignified. I didn't know then exactly what he meant by dignified and I'm not sure he did either. 'Defined a person more,' he said. Where on earth he got all this from I am not sure. Mind you, I do remember that he was going through a funny period. It was about the time that his dad had left home, allegedly with Lily Jordan from Number 11. So maybe, as he was the senior – albeit only – male in the house, he was trying to say something. I don't know.

I do know he was a funny one at times. Everything had to be exactly right. An inch was an inch and not an inch and a bit. Now, I know the importance of that today so I am not scoffing at it. Well, as a painter and decorator with an established reputation – synagogues our speciality – exactness is important. But even then I thought he did push it to the limit. Chocolate bars had to be cut exactly in two – and I mean exactly. So much so that I used to cut mine up and put both hands behind my back so that it was the luck of the draw. But blow me if he didn't say that he was not having that.

'I need to see what I am accepting otherwise it is not on.' And this from a nine-year-old! No amount of explaining or arguing would convince him otherwise. By gum, he was stubborn! Still, he seems to have done all right for himself. You never imagine going to school with a possible future bishop, do you? But the best of luck to him. 'Bishop Thomas' sounds quite refined; or dignified, as he would say. Mind you, I reckon he might have problems with that triangular hat.

Interview D: Dawn and Sharon, two of Thomas' friends from senior school

Dawn and Sharon were two friends who knew Thomas in year ten at Bethsaida Community College where, among other things, they were in the same group for culinary technology (kosher version). This is the first time they have met since they left school. As will be seen from this short interview, objectivity, when the heart is involved, is a difficult achievement.

BRIAN: So, Dawn and Sharon, thank you for seeing me. As I explained in my e-mail, we are expecting a lot of media interest regarding Thomas because of his possible new post in the Christian Church. So we thought it would be good to go to the people who really knew him, particularly in his formative years. All right? So who's going to start? How about you, Sharon?

SHARON: Well, to be honest, Brian, I did know Thomas, but so did many others. He was that kind of person.

DAWN: Oh, come on, Shaz. I used to call her 'Shaz' at school, Brian. If anybody knew him well, you did. Or so you used to tell us.

SHARON: True. But a lot of that was girl talk. I liked to regard me and Thomas as soul mates. I only wish I had realised at the time what an important period of life that is for a developing beta female. My Tai Chi Master was saying this only the other day. It's all right if I read this, isn't it, Brian? You see, it is so real; so now. 'Hidden personal electricity is unfortunately circumvented by hormonal adolescent energy.'

DAWN: I beg your pardon, Shaz! What on earth does that mean?

SHARON: Oh, the same Dawn, eh? You haven't changed, have you? You were always looking for meanings; the surface meanings. The 'skin blips' are not what count. It's what is inner. You see, Thomas was deep. We were deep together.

DAWN: But did you ever snog him?

SHARON: Dawn, you are disgusting!

DAWN: Well, did you?

SHARON: Only once, but it was everlasting.

DAWN: Everlasting?

SHARON: Yes. He was that kind of person. Words and actions were not enough. Nothing was ever taken at face value. There were always things behind things.

DAWN: Like bike sheds.

SHARON: Dawn! Now, you may remember we moved from Bethsaida when I was in year thirteen.

DAWN: Yes, I do. Jerusalem, wasn't it?

SHARON: Downtown Jerusalem. Don't remind me. I remember him asking me why I was going. I explained it was for Dad's job. And he wanted to know what kind of job, what the prospects were for us all and how I would settle. It was quite unselfish in a way but yet somehow more. As if he had to know everything and all the facts before he could accept it.

DAWN: And did you miss him?

SHARON: Looking back, as a soul mate? Oh yes. Like a cedar of Lebanon misses the fertile soil. We had the same karma, you see. But there did remain some outer body connection.

DAWN:	Shaz, I don't mean 'outer body' miss him. I mean *miss* him. You know what I mean.
SHARON:	Dawn! I've told you, you are disgusting.
DAWN:	I know. And?
SHARON:	Yes. Of course I missed him. Still do.
DAWN:	Thought so.

The interview was taped in the Basement Bar at the Hard Rock Cafe, Jerusalem.

Interview E: Mark, Thomas' best friend from university

Mark was from the little village of Dinno, just outside Jerusalem. Thomas used to refer to their friendship as 'genuinely accidental'; even providential. On their first session on the first day of their first year at the City University of Mid-Israel they shared the same work bench in the physics lab. It was friendship at first sight. They remained friends right through university and remain so today. Although Mark has little or no time for his Jewish faith, he respects Thomas in his way of life, though not quite understanding his friend's choice.

We just hit it off right from the start. That sometimes happens, doesn't it? And, to be honest, it was lucky for both of us, because neither of us was really outgoing. I suppose me coming from a little village and experiencing the 'big city' for the first time, and Thomas with his family background... Now, don't get me wrong, there was nothing wrong with it, but I just got the impression that he was pretty sheltered. To a certain extent, it was the perfect preparation for being a scientist, I often felt. And a physicist, at that. He often used to quote his father's phrase: 'If in doubt, doubt.' I have a sneaking suspicion, you know, that, deep down, he had a great admiration for his father, even though he only knew him early on in his life. Mind you, they are the formative years; the time when certainty has not quite given over to questioning doubt.

He used to quote his father quite a bit – apart from the famous 'doubt' one. He once said to me, 'You know, Mark – and this will appeal to you because you are a country lad – my dad once said to me: "Never judge a cow by its face. Always take account of the steam rising from its body." It's worth remembering.'

He never explained what it meant. Mind you, I have a suspicion that his dad never explained it to him, either. All I could think was that he was being warned about taking things at face value and it was important to realise that everybody had a past and a present that was not always obvious, but there were sufficient signs to get to the truth if you were prepared to look and dig. Mind you, it seems that this quotable quote was first uttered a couple of weeks before Mr Rosen left home, so he might have been preparing the way.

Well, you never know, do you? But still, that is his business. Maybe he was trying to tell Thomas something. But, anyway, whatever it was, it certainly had an effect on him because there was no way our Thomas was taking anything at face value.

In our second year, we shared a house together and he decided to get some of that flat-pack furniture from Ikea. Well you had to see him to believe it. Putting it together was almost an art form – well, it would have been if he had been an artist. I used to joke with him that if the manufacturers only knew, not only would they supply a couple of extra screws and some more of those wooden peg things but they would include an extra identical book of instructions. He would read the instructions, then follow them and then, when he had finished building, read them again. I wouldn't mind but it was only a rack for the *Radio Times*. But that was him: thorough to a fault. He took nothing for granted; checked everything out.

I'm not quite sure what being a bishop involves but if it is about being a man who is only comfortable with certainty and to a certain extent can be in control of his own destiny then I reckon he will make a good one. I'm not sure if Ikea do new cathedrals – hopefully not, for everyone's sake.

Interview F: Thomas' fellow Apostle, James the Less

James the Less was Thomas' best friend among the Apostles. In fact, each of them got fairly limited coverage in the four Gospels. Thomas is really only known for his famous doubting experience and James is simply known by the title 'Less' to distinguish him from the other James, brother of John, son of Zebedee, and later Bishop of Jerusalem. Against those achievements it would seem obvious why this man is called James the Less – though in fact it was a height thing.

Let me say, first of all, that I am very pleased to write these few words about my good friend Thomas. I know some people find it difficult to accept that among the 'gang of twelve', as we were known by some, there can be close friendships. But that was the case. And it is my experience that, rather than being divisive, an honest, good friendship can really add to the strength and the influence of any group. And our friendship was an honest good one. With me at five foot seven and Thomas six foot two, extreme height was initially the common factor. It was Judas who coined the phrase 'Little and Large', after a music hall turn he'd seen some years previously.

To understand Thomas, you had to understand his thinking. Dealing with bits of metal and bits of steel and lumps of wood he was OK. There were rules for them and things obeyed rules. But with people, he used to say, 'Every one is a whole new ball game'. He once quoted me something his father had said about a cow and steam rising from it. Still don't understand it to this day but it obviously made an impression on him.

I suppose what you are interested in is the famous 'doubting' scene. If you have read Thomas' version, you will see where he is coming from. You may not agree but you would have to sympathise with him. And really you had to be there to appreciate what it was like. Windows and doors were locked shut; we were cut off from the outside world, but not from rumours, not from text messages. 'Jesus had not really died,' some said. 'He had died but had risen again,' claimed others. Some people claimed they had seen him. Others thought they had. Someone even suggested he had a twin brother who had lived all his life in Nazareth until now. And so on. So you see, that was the situation Thomas left when he went out to the shops. So can you really blame him for being a bit sceptical when he returned? Plus, remember his background. As he used to say to me, 'Jimmy, it's not as easy as people think. I can't suddenly switch off being a scientist just because I have become an Apostle. It's a very different approach, what with faith and all. But I am working at it.'

And I knew he was. And, of course, we know what happened. Thomas, 'the doubter', in fact became the first person to actually acknowledge Christ's divinity with the famous 'My Lord and my God'.

It's strange when you think about it. Also, what was never reported was that, despite our differences on many things not one person, and definitely not Jesus, ever said: 'I told you so'. Now, that for me says two things: one, we were a genuinely close-knit group who could easily absorb any – and I mean any – individual faults, whether it was doubting or denying or even suicide (I only wish Judas had come to us first); and, secondly, it reminded us all that to be an Apostle did not mean neutering our personality or way of approaching things: scientist or artist, comedian or bore. Thomas, by remaining Thomas, helped us all as a group. He is a great man, a great friend, and I have no doubts he will make a great bishop.

Interview G: Dolores Greenhalgh, a parishioner of St Gabriel's, Tiberias

Miss Greenhalgh is an unmarried sixty-seven-year-old woman. She worked in the civil service accounts department in Tiberias and was involved in setting up the Gift Aid programme for St Gabriel's. She regards herself as a kind of mentor to Fr Tom, whom she has always said doesn't look after himself properly and eats too many pre-cooked meals from Marks & Spencer's. Fr Tom smiles at her frequent advice. She was not available for interview but wrote the following letter.

Dear Mr Levy,

Thank you very much for your kind letter, which arrived only yesterday by the dinnertime post. I hope you do not think that such a swift response represents non-thinking haste. Nothing could be further from the truth. You see, there is so much I could write about Father Tom that it really is a question of not where to start but where to stop. Such a lovely man and, if he does become bishop, which Cecil our sacristan says is a strong possibility, all I can say is that it will be our parish's loss and the Church's gain. It's funny; but, as I am sure you know – because you do sound like a clever man from your letter – Fr Tom was at St Philomena's in Cana before he came to St Gabriel's. That's where my sister, Brigid, lives and when she heard he was coming to us she said we were lucky because he was a lovely man. And he is.

What I like about him is that he is always interested in people, especially us little people. Now, I have always done the altar laundry. My mother used to do it for Father Wilfrid and I continued when she died. May the Lord have mercy on her soul (and, of course, on Father Wilfrid's). Now, when Fr Tom came he asked me if I was happy to continue. Well, of course, I said I was, and that I regarded it as an honour to do such a thing for Almighty God. Well, he said, this was fine but he didn't want to assume anything. That was him, not taking anything for granted.

You see, Fr Tom is man who likes things in order and, when a thing goes wrong, if he knows how it works he will know how to fix it. He doesn't like to leave anything to chance. I remember one parish council meeting. It must have been just after he had arrived. He questioned each of us on almost every single aspect concerning the parish. It was like *Mastermind,* where we all had our chosen topic. He needed to know everything about the liturgy and the Christmas fair, who was the service engineer for the church boiler and who supplied the newsletter; everything. As I say, we all stayed with him through all that and, to be honest, most of us are glad we did. Because that is him, a man of detail for which everything must have a reason. Organised. But, for me, his greatest strength is that he is never afraid to admit when he is wrong. No ifs or buts. Simply, 'I am sorry'.

In a way, that is the mixture of the man: someone who needs the facts and the reasons, who likes to leave nothing to chance, but knows sometimes he has to. One of his favourite phrases as he draws something to a conclusion is: 'Right, well, that is that settled then.' But I often feel that under his breath he is saying 'At least, I hope so.' As if he has memories.

Anyway, Mr Levy, I hope this is the kind of thing you were looking for. Sorry I don't seem to have mentioned many negative things but there don't seem to be many. He is a lovely man.

Yours faithfully in Our Lord and his mother,

Dolores Greenhalgh (Miss)

Interview H: James, the Apostle, Bishop of Jerusalem

James was the first Bishop of Jerusalem of the newly-formed Christian Church. In those early days it soon dawned on the Apostles that, once Jesus had left them, there would be some scope for people from their own group to get some of the top jobs. With this in mind, money would have been laid on James. Although the incident when the mother of James and John had pushed her sons towards Jesus in the famous 'but can they drink the chalice I will drink?' incident was well known, it was later thought that it was really James that had put her up to it. John was a different character altogether. However, from a positive point of view, there is never any fault in a person recognising how good they are. I suggest that might be James' argument.

Let me first put on record how delighted I am to contribute to this small symposium on my very good friend Father Thomas. He is a fine man and I would like to think that everything that follows simply elucidates those few powerful words: he is a fine man.

As you possibly know, his was not the easiest of childhoods. To a few of us who knew him so well, he sometimes referred to himself as 'Thomas the Twin'. Sadly, Teresa, for that was indeed her name, did not survive early infanthood and this was one of the ways Thomas liked to ensure she would not be forgotten. Yes, he is a fine man.

Unfortunately, Thomas will go down in history as the famous 'Doubter'. This is a tremendous tragedy, really, as he was much more than that. I am pleased to see that elsewhere in this little tome he explains his reasons for what really was an unfortunate misunderstanding and something that definitely did not merit his deplorable treatment by the tabloid press. But I am afraid that is the world we live in. I remember being involved in a similar so-called scandal when Mother was reputed to have approached Jesus on mine and my brother's behalf regarding what we could offer our brethren in the way of humble service. The whole incident definitely did not merit the headline 'Jobs for the Boys?' It was utterly scandalous.

Since I have been honoured by Pope Peter to be the first Bishop of Jerusalem, I have always striven to recognise in those of my flock – laity and well as clerical – the God-given talents they have and how best they can use those talents for the up-building of our little, growing, Christian community.

In this regard, I would like to put on record my gratitude to my cousin Albert and his wife Louisa for being instrumental in ensuring that a proper image of the Church, and obviously of me as shepherd of the flock, is portrayed. Actually, it was they themselves who brought to my notice this little booklet and suggested I might wish to contribute. I, of course, was overjoyed at the suggestion and only hope I have done my good friend Father Thomas credit in these few words.

This brings me neatly to my conclusion and my overriding view that Father Thomas is a fine man and I am sure that he will continue to be of great benefit to the Church, either remaining as a parish priest or if he is elevated to Bishop of one of the smaller, newly-founded dioceses in our country.

With these few words goes my sincere apostolic blessing to all who may read them.

A Life Built on Water

*Incidents from Peter's life
Told by one of his best friends*

At the shop

So there I was, sitting in my shop doing the *Guardian* crossword while waiting for a consignment of birthstones to arrive. I hadn't a clue what to expect. It was my cousin, who owned Emporium Moab in Bethany, who had told me they were the latest thing. I believed him. He had never been wrong before. I mean, thanks to him, I was the first person in Bethsaida selling Rubik's Cubes and lava lamps. I know they are old hat now but that was not the case back in those days.

Suddenly, old Mrs Abrahams from Café Israel came in and told me that Simon Peter had been killed. Apparently he was crucified. 'And, what's more, upside down!' she said. 'And do you know, when—'

I stopped her there as I could see she was on a roll and I am not good with details. Before long, I'd have felt I was playing a limp-on part in *Casualty*. So I said, 'You are joking?' (Funny how we say that isn't it, when it obviously is not a joking matter.) I went on, 'Just leave me, please. But thank you.' I possibly said this a little too brusquely, but it was the shock, you see. And I did need to be alone. Well, I mean, it's not every day your best friend is crucified; and upside down. I actually closed the shop. Well, you do, don't you? And, what's more, I turned the lights off inside to give a sombre atmosphere. I hoped my birthstones would be delivered next door.

Saintly sinner

Simon Peter and me had fished next to each other for the best part of twenty years before he went off to follow that Messiah,

Jesus. You've heard of him, haven't you? He was a strange man. Now, don't get me wrong, I would not talk ill of the dead. As you know, Jesus was crucified as well; head up, though. And now Simon Peter had been crucified upside down. I bet that was his idea – something to do with not being worthy and all that. Although he became Jesus' right-hand man, with more or less right of succession, he never quite felt up to it. He was a strange mixture, even though I say it myself. My wife always used to call him 'the saintly sinner'. And he always used to laugh and give the same response, 'Eh, Miriam, not so much of the saintly! You'll be making me like your husband.'

Question of denial

Mind you, Simon Peter had his problems; or at least some people said so. For example, the night before Jesus was crucified he is supposed to have actually denied he had ever heard of the man when challenged by some young slip of a waitress. Now, if you'd seen the size of him you'd think the whole thing laughable. And, to be honest, my immediate reaction was to regard it as such. But you never know, do you? People do funny things when their backs are to the wall. They don't always act in the way they would if they had more time. And, the more I have thought about it over the years, the more I reckon there might be something in it. You see, the person who told me about it also said they'd found Simon Peter later on in a side alley crying his eyes out; like a baby. Now, I know he was a man who didn't easily cry. Well, you don't, do you? Fishermen are tough. But the more I have thought about it, the more possibilities seem to slip into place.

Question of apology

It would tie up in so far as he was definitely into saying sorry. He used to go on about forgiving people not seven times but seventy times seven. Now, I know that was Jesus talk but Simon Peter seemed really taken in by it, as if it were one of the linchpins of what his friend was all about. You never know, maybe he did feel an apology to Jesus was in order but impossible in the circumstances, so he had to get it out of his system somehow. I suppose that might account for the crying business. You can never tell, can you? I'm rambling, aren't I? But it's all been such a shock. You see, as well as Simon Peter being a really good friend, if it had not been for him I wouldn't have had my shop. It goes back a bit. Have you got time? Right then.

Boat minder

As I said earlier, we fished side by side for the best part of twenty years. There was me and my brother Andrew, and him and his brother Andrew. We had good, healthy competition, but also respect between us. Simon Peter was a tough man, but fair. Quick-tempered would be an understatement. And if he felt he was right, there was no stopping him. Not the brightest crystal in the chandelier but straight as a die; and convincingly honest. He's the only man I have ever known to talk his way out of a parking ticket. And then, when Peter and Andrew left to follow Jesus, he sold me their boat. It was market price but really a steal. But that was him: rough and blunt, but as sentimental as a piece of wet cheese. He said he would like their boat to go to a good home. So I promised to look after it as if it were my own: wash it and feed it with new paint regularly.

Aladdin's cave

And then, three years later, I had my accident – again, I don't do medical details. I sold the boat and my own and set up this little gift shop: Aladdin's Cave. It had no name when I opened so I promised my suppliers that I would call it after the person who gave me the best commission. Well, this chap turned up, kind of Egyptian-looking, selling these lamps. They were a bit green and mouldy, but I bought a job lot with the intention of cleaning them up. I mentioned this to the Egyptian. Well, he nearly fell out of his tree. 'Don't polish them,' he said, 'whatever you do. It'll bring bad luck. At least!' So I just left them all in a wicker basket near the door and I sell them as antiques. They go like hot cakes. People round here like a bit of culture. I also stock shells and maritime memorabilia. That was Simon Peter's idea.

Dependable

And now he is dead; crucified upside down. I still can't believe it. You see, that would never have happened if he had remained a fisherman. I know drowning is no joke but it's not as bad as crucifixion; whichever way up. Mind you, listening to some of the things Jesus used to talk about, it was always on the cards. I don't mean they were encouraged to look forward to death or anything, no way, but rather to accept whatever came their way. It was about trusting, depending on God and those around you. And that was definitely the case with Simon Peter. His word was his bond. I suppose that is one of the things that made us friends. Well, I am a bit like that myself; you have to be, especially if you are working with others.

Water walk

One of the things I always admired about Simon Peter was the way he was completely upfront when talking about Jesus. He made no bones about how he admired him and how he didn't always see what he was getting at but was prepared to give it time. Two incidents really stick out. He told me about the first and I was there at the second.

Apparently, one day, a few of them were out in their boat, crossing over from one side of the lake to the other. Jesus suddenly appeared, apparently walking on the water. Now, Simon Peter was so taken by this he asked if he could get out of the boat and walk across and join him. I reckon he said this for a joke, you know, because he had a funny sense of humour. And Jesus simply said: 'Be my guest'. Well he said he was OK at the beginning but then, when he felt the wind get up, he started to panic a bit and began to sink. I always found that strange because I am sure if it were me the wind wouldn't bother me, but the thought of the few fathoms of water beneath me definitely would. Anyway, the upshot was that Jesus simply reached out and grabbed his hand. So, in a way, you could say that Jesus saved Simon Peter's life. But from another point of view you could say it was a set-up. Weird. But it definitely impressed my friend. Mind you, nothing like as much as the other occasion. And I was there for that.

Say no to Moonies

It was early one morning on the lake. Oh, by the way, before I go on I would like to make a couple of things clear. Don't get me wrong about the influence that Jesus had on my friend. It wasn't like the Moonies or anything. There was no question of Jesus zoning in on simple working folk and convincing them by tricks. No way. If I have given that impression, I am sorry. And I apologise. What I know about Jesus is that he was an honest man and always seemed to be looking out for the good of others. I must admit I found some of his statements a bit OTT – like the seventy times seventy apologies business and letting people beat you up and not retaliating and things – but generally he was good. And from what Simon Peter told me, and I know he was truthful about this, it was the everyday, ordinary, normal things that made Jesus attractive. Sorry if I have gone on a bit about that but I do want to be fair to Jesus and also to my friend, Simon Peter, especially as neither of them can speak up for themselves any longer; being dead and all that.

Bad night

So, where was I? Oh, yes, this particular morning. Now, first of all you need to know that it was an accepted fact that Simon Peter was the best fisherman among all of us. He could read the waters as clearly as you or I could read the front page of *The Sun* or *The Mirror*. Having said that, we all have bad days, and bad nights. And this was one of them. We were out there all night and caught nothing. That's if you discount a mountain bike frame, a car inner tube and a Kwik Save trolley. Then Jesus appeared on the shore. By 'appeared' I don't mean like from nowhere, like Dr Who or anything, I mean we were suddenly aware of him being there. Well, he asked us if we had caught anything. Now a question like that made you realise why he was a Messiah and not a fisherman because, as we were still so high in the water, it should have been obvious.

Good morning

But listen to this. When Simon Peter said "Fraid not, but you can't win 'em all', Jesus suggested that Simon Peter try the other side of the boat, to throw his net there. Well, I wouldn't say it was a silly suggestion, more like ridiculous.

But blow me, without a murmur, Simon Peter simply said: 'Of course, Jesus. Why didn't I think of that?' There was hardly a trace of sarcasm. And he did it. Now, I had never taken Simon Peter for a drinker but at that point I did wonder whether his ruddy face was not just from cold, watery fishing trips. But, before I could comment, the cry went up 'Fish adeck aboard' (a local cry). I couldn't believe it and was only grateful Simon Peter and Andrew had invested in the new nylon nets that had just come out. They're not strictly legal in the European Union but, of course, that did not affect us. Well, it took all of us to pull the nets to shore. Crazy. I'm still not sure how it happened. I mean, I know you get these people in some of the nightclubs in Jerusalem who make buildings vanish and saw women in half but this was different. And really, from that morning, Simon Peter was never the same again.

A suitable name

And now he has been crucified; upside down. And all because he gave up fishing and followed Jesus. Mind you, I reckon I can live with that; which is more than he can. People have to follow what they believe is right. Men of principle attract men of principle. And there's no doubt Jesus and Simon Peter definitely fitted into that category. It will just take a bit of getting used to that Simon Peter is dead. I suppose, as a mark of respect, I could rename my shop after him. I must think of a suitable name.

Printed in the United States
79407LV00001B/105